Heiden Hexology,
Essays and Interviews
by
Hunter M. Yoder

First published in 2012 by
Zaubereigarten/ The Hex Factory
2080 East Cumberland Street
Philadelphia, Pa 19125
www.thehexfactory.com

Copyright 2012 Hunter M. Yoder
All rights reserved. No part of this publication may be reproduced or transmitted in any form or by any means, electronic or mechanical, including photocopying, scanning, recording, or by any information storage and retrieval system, without permission in writing from Hunter M. Yoder. Reviewers may quote brief passages.
Updated 01/2014

I dedicate this book to the memory of the Hexologists of Berks County, Pennsylvania, Milton Hill, Johnny Ott, Johnny Claypoole, and a special dedication to the memory of Lee R. Gandee, Hexenmeister

Contributors

The words and images of the following appear in the essays and interviews in addition to my own which make up this book:

O. Henrietta Fisher
Jeff Grandmason, (Valúlfr Vaerulsson, Der Waldzauberer)
Alison Grandmason (Swanhilde)
Troy Wisehart
Patrick Donmoyer
Eric Claypoole
Gandvaldr Bláskikkja
Paul Waggener, (Grimnir)
Matthias Waggener
Orva Gaile Clubb
Erika Yoder
Brigitte Yoder
Gloria Dillard Brown
Sarah Elizabeth Smith Eppihimer
Amber Faith
Patricia Hall
Jakob Brunner
Arrowyn Craban Lauer
Aaron Badger
Rebecca Radcliff
Krystal Anderson
Mike Babbish
Pia Fontaine, (Lady Sunshine MoonRaven)
Dennis Boyer

5

Table of Contents

Preface..8
Essays...11
Location Sign Devices..12
Towards Defining a Heathen Hexology Berks County Eight Pointed Star and the Black Sun (Schwarze Sonne), 2009............15
The Swastika and the Cross, 2009......................................17
Scalloping and Emanation in Hexology, 2009....................19
Rotational Aspects of Bindrunes in Hexology, 2009..........21
Deitsch Heathen Hexology Show, at Germ Bookstore, 2009.....22
Galdrastafir and Hexology, 2010..26
Runic Symbology in Contemporary Deitsch Hexology, by Hunter Yoder 29
Magic Plants Used Symbolically in Germanic Heathen Hexology, 2010..49
The Reanimation of Germanic Tribalism in PA Deitsch Hexology, 2010..70
Six Questions to Six Heathen Hexologists and their Six Hexes 105
    Interviews..129
Hunter Yoder Interview with Valulfr Vaerulsson, 2008 130
Waldzauberer Interview with Hunter Yoder 141
Interview with Hexenfrau Swanhilde with Hunter Yoder..........155
....155
Eric Claypoole, Berks County Hexologist Interview with Hunter Yoder 168
    Patrick Donmoyer, Berks County Hexologist and Scholar ..182
Interview with Grímnir with Hunter Yoder, 2009.....................204
Gandvaldr Bláskikkja Interview with Hunter Yoder..................212
Troy Wisehart Interview with Hunter Yoder..............................224
Orva Gaile Clubb nee Price Interview with Hunter Yoder.........238
O.Henrietta Fisher Interview with Hunter Yoder 279
    O.Henrietta interviews Hunter Yoder for the show,"In Between the Sheets at the Hex Factory, Hunter Yoder and O. Henrietta Fisher" 295

Reviews at the Hex Factory..308
Between the Sheets 310
O. Henrietta and Hunter Yoder at the Hex Factory....................310
Heiden Hexology in Oley, PA......................................320
Gottinen und Heiden Hexology..325

Preface

The book you are about to read documents the recent events in the evolution of a Pennsylvania German or Deitsch magical folk art known as Hexology. These signs are called Barnstars, Hex signs, Hexezeeche, Hexefoos and so on. The form is on a branch of the family tree of Pennsylvania German Folk Art along with works on paper known as Fraktur and the art of scissor cutting or Scherenschnitte.
Recent interest in Pennsylvania German Folk Magic driven by the internet has led to the transformation of this formerly conservative quiet Protestant grandmother's legacy to an amped up Pagan/ Heathen/ Heiden, rejection of Western Civilization, and monotheism.
As the gateway to most of North America for all of the German immigration, Pennsylvania retains the kultur and residual ancestral energies of the single largest minority that until recently has been invisible. Those of German ancestry have learned to be silent about their heritage. In America's so called multicultural approach to ethnicity, those of European ancestry have been trained to refer to themselves as mongrels. This policy along with the recent worldwide economic collapse provided the catalyst for many of those 'mongrels' to review this ethnic status and in doing so the blinders have fallen from their eyes.. It is during this period, roughly 2008 through 2012 that this book was written.
It is important to understand that Hexology alone did not have the strength to bring about this astonishing

transformation of this disenfranchised minority. It was the coupling of Hexology with the Elder Futhark of Runes, the old pre Christian magical alphabet of Northern Europe that has had such a dramatically powerful effect. Icelandic magic and Pennsylvania German Hexology are kissing cousins. The unification of the galdrstave with the hexezeeche yielded astonishing results included in this book. The when and where this occurred is not clear, but what is clear is my personal effort in this direction which makes up the contents of this book. I published in HEX MAGAZINE, in the Fall & Winter of 2008, the essay RUNIC SYMBOLOGY IN CONTEMPORARY DEITSCH HEXOLOGY, which is included here in this volume. And the rest is history. The ripple effect that was felt throughout the Germanic Heathen community has been significant. Rune schools are now including Hexology in their curriculum.

Tribalism, ancestor worship and creation myths resonate on a deeper level then the monotheisms that dominate western civilization. This lack of a tribal identity for those of European descent has led to the idealization of the Indigenous peoples. By romanticizing the primitive cultures, those in the West can vicariously belong to something they lack in the cold materialistic, secular, multicultural, monokultur world they live in. In particular, shamanism has become the darling of new age enlightenment. I was fortunate to grow up in the Deitsch kultur and have come to realize that there is no need to adopt the ways of the Indigenous tribes.

Pennsylvania German folk magic is the oldest continuous tradition brought over from Europe in North America. The Pennsylvania Germans taught the Indigenous it was not a one way learning experience as is generally accepted particularly in the areas of horiculture and the healing arts. The early German settlers in Pennsylvania were Christians. However as Guido Von List stated, this Christianity retained and preserved the ancient Germanic tribal ways. Lets face it, the Barnstars of Berks County, Pa certainly don't look very Christian, in fact it is important to understand that the Plain sects, the Mennonites and the more extreme Amish never decorate their barns with these signs. They are fully aware that these signs are witchcraft. The word for witch in German is Hex. Witchcraft is Hexerei. While witchcraft in colonial New England was vigorously eradicated, in Pennsylvania it prospered. The Commonwealth of Pennsylvania issued licenses for practicing Brauchers until the notorious York County Hex Murder in 1929. The Deitsch kultur has been the talisman, the Hex if you will ,that has protected those of German descent from eternal damnation by the vestigial monotheism and the newer 'multiculturalism' that denied them a voice. No longer just a quaint folk art form, the new Heiden Hexology is effecting their lives today. Anyone with the will to do so can participate and as you are about to see, they have.

Hunter Yoder, 04/11/2012

Essays

Location Sign Devices

Hunter Yoder, 1976

The function of the brightly decorative Hex Signs seen on local barns may serve a purpose other then 'chust fer nice' They seem to not only be in this particular geographical locale (Berks County) but may serve as pointers to particular places of importance in the area. In driving from the Kutztown area in a roughly northeast direction towards the Blue Mountains, the Hex Signs encountered along the way change notably as one becomes closer to the Mountains.

The Hex Signs in northern Berks County are mostly based on the eight pointed star which characteristically has a red circle for a center. Usually they have two concentric circles with a regressive star pattern, star within a star and so forth. The eight pointed star is based on multiplying the cardinal points by two. The border surrounding the 'star' varies from radiating lines resembling snakes to tight geometric triangular halos. The border becomes the place of the most extensive variation from barn to barn. And as the movement from the great valley nothward to the Blue Mountains proceeds, the borders become notably more complex and agitated. Generally, the borders of Hex Signs near the Mountains are based on a triangular motif which consists of painted triangular shapes alternating with hatched triangles which may indicate a clockwise or counterclockwise spin.

The centers also take on a different more developed aspect. The central red dot which is the small circle usually painted red, dead center in the basic Hex Sign now may be come a Hex Sign within a Hex Sign, a reflection of itself within itself.

This aspect of Hexology is an important one in determining what the purpose these things may have and their relation to the ambient environment. For example, there is a barn located between Kutztown, PA and the tourist attraction, Crystal Cave which has sixteen pointed stars and a complex triangular border complete with hatchings on its Hex Signs. It is peculiar in the immediate area where most of the Hexes painted on the barns are only the simpler eight pointed star variety with painted radiating snake-like lines radiating outward. This would be in Richmond Township, Berks County. This particular barn which stands out, has all the elements in its Hex Signs as those which are at least ten miles north, near Kempton, Pa. This barn is situated on the corner of the road near the top of a hill. Driving in one direction, one approaches the barn from the top of the hill going down, the 'Signs' standout, confronting the viewer. One becomes dazzled by their presence and then after making the oncoming bend in the road they become lost from sight. Immediately afterward, the viewer is treated to a beautiful panoramic view of the

Blue Mountains, in particular the highest point in Berks County, the Pinnacle, which juts out very distinctly from the Appalachian Mountain Ridge. Coming up the road from the opposite direction, one sees nothing unless he cranes his neck.

The author believes that what the Hex Signs are doing in this particular example is to relay the attention attracting ability of high points and reflect that energy in a visual language and in a sense eliminate the ten mile distance between the barn and the mountains. The Hexes become points of self projection from afar. Familiarity with the landscape may lead to knowledge of that distant indicated point (the Pinnacle) when one is there looking back in the direction of that faraway painted barn. The experience for the author cuts through time and space allowing him to be simultaneously two places at the same moment. The thinking here is that this was the intention of the style and placement of the Hexes.

Towards Defining a Heathen Hexology Berks County Eight Pointed Star and the Black Sun (Schwarze Sonne), 2009

May be of interest to point out some of the striking similarities between the Hexafuus that is found most commonly in Berks County and the the Deutsch Black Sun, also called 'Schwarze Sonne' The most striking similarity is the the sixteen or twelve radiating vectors used in yellow and black in the center. Also the indication of spin by the twelve Sowilo runes. Deitsch hexology employees both the sixteen and the twelve always in black yellow and white with a red center. Indication of the the rotation is indicated in the border in a variety of ways, radiation outward in Greenwich township is indicated by black rays of sun in a snake like design, the more the merrier and the more the merrier if
the location of the site is in plain view of the Mountains, one in particular, the Pinnacle, Berks County's highest and strangest point.

The so called Migration age Alemannic decorative brooches were worn by the women around their waists and this speaks not of a death sun, or a hate sun but rather a tribal symbol, our Tribe. It symbolizes to me fertility, successful coupling, a fat bountiful life. Its important that we distinquish this from the prostitution of that symbol for perverted political purposes.

As Germanic descendants, we can bask in the warmth of our
Tribal 'schwarze sonne' The wheel had as profound effect on our ancestors as the internet/computer technology of our current era. The wheel was the vehicle which allowed the tribes to move and conquer from the Black Sea into all of Europe. Its mystical connection to the sun or "Sonnenrad' is essential to an understanding of our Indo European tribal origins. It functions as both a destroyer and a giver of life and this is dependent upon rotational values on a purely 'sigil' level.

The Swastika and the Cross, 2009

The swastika is just a kind of cross. Its a cross that indicates spin. Equilateral crosses indicate a point and are static, they may remain motionless while the rest of the cosmos moves. A swastika is abit more sophisticated in their indication of clockwise or counterclockwise motion.
In Hexerei, Germanic witchcraft, the practice of healing is
frequently accompanied or sealed with the indication of three crosses. The direction of the crossing indicates a giving or taking in the intention. We get this from Lee R. Gandee,
"In any benevolent work, the crosses are made by closing the right hand into a fist. Using the thumb, first make a downward stroke, then raise the hand to the right and cross the first stroke horizontally toward the left. The use of the left hand and a crossing from the left to right is for malevolent purposes-useful when one is cursing a malevolent condition"
page 117 "Strange Experience"

The left handed cross is not bad and the right handed good, they are relative to the intention. The same is true of the swastika, the counter clockwise, the one most commonly seen in the Hindu and Buddhist traditions is not good and the
clockwise one commonly associated with National

Socialism, bad.

In the Hexology, The sun is central to fertility and abundance on the farm as is the rain. The two are most commonly seen together on the Berks County 8 pointed star, Gandee calls the Earthstar. In Berks County it really is a 'sun' star. As such the crossed Sowilo runes make the wheel turn and I use it in the very center in red. The direction of spin maybe with or counter to the surrounding elements in the Hexezeeche.

Scalloping and Emanation in Hexology, 2009

We have been told that the scalloping around the circumference of a hexafoos is to promote "smooth sailing in life" This from Jacob Zook, Johnny Ott's Business partner.
What is he talking about really? A more in depth look at the energetic flow in this matter reveals that "smooth sailing through life" is a kenning for the emanation outward
of the hexafoos's intent. If the scalloping is repeated outwardly, it becomes clear. This is done as well in the Yantra, for instance:
http://www.exoticindiaart.com/artimages/cosmos.jpg
The scalloping is in a sense like the result of throwing a stone into a still pond, they would be the unending outward moving ripples in this metaphor.

Sunnawendi Stave, 2010

Rotational Aspects of Bindrunes in Hexology, 2009

As a note and a part of our ongoing work here. I would like to mention the importance of the rotational and counter rotational aspects of creating bindrunes in the Hexology.

Generally the Bindrune is the center of a Hexezeeche and as so is indicated by its geometrical center in the cosmos, usually a crossing of some sort, an indication of a point, in other traditions such as the Yantra this would be the Bindu.......

I have found that, when creating a Bindrune center it is optimized by the addition of counter rotational spins on elements that unify to create the center, (Bindrune)

Counter rotations work exactly in the same way as an "X" works only with the additional energy of rotational movement. This make it a more dynamic structure and insures its reverberation into the 'Living Universe'

The quandary has always been, do you want to reinforce a rotational movement throughout by keeping the rotational direction in all the elements the same?

I think that by crossing the directions in the center the question answers itself.

Deitsch Heathen Hexology Show, at Germ Bookstore, 2009

Rabbits are fully capable of producing their young with totally different fathers siring individual kits. This is also true of the Pennsylvania German practice of producing Hex signs.
The Deitsch Heathen Hexology show this past winter at GERM Bookstore/Gallery is evidence of an ancient all father as the sire of this show.
Although the Deitsch kultur has been essentially xtian with elements of Folk Religion that are not in any doctrine set forth by any church or organized religion, The Hexology of the PA Germans has always been generally accepted from the advent of German European settlers to the present day as being merely decorative, or "chust for nice"
More recent Heathen influences have rediscovered their Germanic roots in these energized earthstars. Swanhilde, der Waldzaubere, Patricia Hall and myself, Hunter Yoder explored this rediscovered territory in the show of 32 Hexes.
The location for this historic show was appropriately in Philadelphia, the port of entry for the ancestors into this country and Pennsylvania of the Heathen Hexologists included in the show.
So this was not merely another 'art show' This was an extenstion of an ancient folk art tradition, tribal in nature and as such resonated with the largely Northern European derived community of Fishtown where it was

shown.

Individual self expression was restricted to a stylized idiom largely of six and eight pointed stars with circles. Swanhilde and der Waldzauberer, founders of the Rune School the Wolfbund, found something about the Hexology/Hexerei of Berks county that called to their ancestral blood. No runes were overtly visible in their work.

Patricia Hall, from Philadelphia adapted xtian fraktur and hexology replacing the monotheistic elements with bindrunes and heathen symbology. The results were astounding.......The overt heathen imagery made the simplicity of the Hexes surge with unreserved power. As for myself, the first time I used a "Helm of Awe" in the center of a Berks County 8 pointed Hex earthstar, in 2007, I knew it was off to the races.

David E Williams, receives here a well deserved credit for his bizarre venue largely because it is unapologetically Germanic, perhaps the origin of the name, Germ. His Church of Satan sensibility is quite compatible with the reemerging heathenism.

Mr Williams has responded to my characterization of his sensibilities as such:

"Well, that's a stretch, but YOUR are writing the article not me. And I know you've always expressed these sentiments in person, so you might as well keep it in. Especially with the HEX mag readership!

I am not nor have I ever been a member of the Church of Satan, so this would be a weird inaccuracy, for sure. I know some members -- including the current High Priest -- but again, I'm not a member.

Otherwise, it's a nice encapsulation. I hope she chooses to publish it. I mean, it had to be THE Germanic Heathen art event of the year... at least so far!"

Hunter M. Yoder, Patricia Hall, David E. Williams, Valulfr Vaerulsson, Swanhilde at the Opening of Deitsch Heathen Hexology, 02/2009

Galdrastafir and Hexology, 2010

Viewing the Icelandic Galdrastafir from a Hexological perspective is an inevitable part of the current evolution in the metaphysical thought patterns of this site. Hexology is more of a 'mechanical' how do these things work and how can they be used as tiny metaphysical machines which differs from a more 'magical' Hexerei or Galdr perspective.

The ones that are the easiest to work with would be the radiating from a central point such as the Helm of Awe. They tend to go as 'aights' the Northern divisor in all things including the units of measurement and of course the Runes. The 'Earthstar' of Hexology is no different. However unlike Hexology, the "Helm" in all its variants uses, additional components on each ray. Most frequently there is the cross hatch, usually three per ray. These I intuit as multipliers, three hatches three times the power of each ray. The point of each ray in the Helm, is forked into three, this works as an Algiz Rune and there are aight of those.....a bindrune. The forking also works simply as a director of flow outward. Three is a very powerful configuration and predates the 'three stooges' by many millenia, lol. but there is quite the sort of energy in Larry, Curly, and Moe that fits the bill here. Its not three of the same its like basic alternating current, a hot, a neutral and a ground, and without all three there is no flow. So the cross hatching interacts with the fork as a three times three times 8 or seventy two or as a three times eight times three or a one hundred ninety two, both very potent magnitudes of energy. Variants on the forks go either cupped forks or straight forks. Cupped ones would direct a more intense flow in the direction of the ray much like a spotlight, the straight fork would act more like a flood light from the central point or fyr.

Variants on the straight cross hatches are cupped cross marks and circles. The cupped marks either are curve inward or outward. By utilizing these cupping device energy is either focused outward or it deflects alien negative energy from the center.

Hexology is almost always concerned with either an outward flow for an intention or prevention of a destructive flow inward for protection. It rarely mixes the two but that may change soon.

Other Galdrastafir are oriented in a 'tree like' configuration, hence the name Galdrastafir. They are upright verticals with branches, sometimes symmetrical sometimes not. These are more complex in that they may employ several 'Helm like' radiating figures connected by the branches of the 'tree' Typically one of these radiating components dominates the others. They operate as cosmograms and like a computer, configured to meet personal needs or objectives. Some are relatively simply others quite complex and grow into elaborate configurations used as a kind of circuitry in the metaphysical plane. They probably employ 'tricks' to prevent a straightforward reading and to retain the core like intention without outward corruption. They have 'spyware' built in. In this manner are structurally more complex then our simple Hexafoos. Hexerei utilizes other means to prevent tampering, usually in a more earthy manner. However the structural definition of these 'trees' has an appeal to this author.

Curiously, Runes and bindrunes are used sparingly in these things and the utilization of primal geometric forms tend to be of more use. If hooked crosses or fyrfos are employed, rotational values become a dynamic aspect of the overall intent. Other devices employed might be diagonal branches which may have directional values moving toward or away from radiating components, say a from above on the right to below on the left or visa versa. These may operate in the same way clockwise and counter clockwise values do on the fyrfos, namely clockwise values are positive and counter clockwise values negative. This is not to say that the Galdrastafir is good or bad but rather the way in which it is oriented to achieve success.

Finally, you will hear time and time again from Rune 'scholars' of the interplay between a subjective universe as a center and the manifestation of intent from there into a objective universe. Personally that sort of simplistic dualistic explanation fails to take into the account the irrationality of a manifest universe these things create if they are really good. No such explanation is needed as long as the desired intent works!

Runic Symbology in Contemporary Deitsch Hexology, by Hunter Yoder

originally published, HEX MAGAZINE, Fall & Winter 2008, Issue 4

'Virginville Helm, 2007' Hunter Yoder

Hexology differs from Hexerei, which is used to describe the collected practices of Germanic witchcraft. Hexology refers specifically to the practice of creating what Lee Gandee describes as "Painted Prayers," or Hex signs. In the Pennsylvania Deitsch dialect, they are called Hexafoos (witch's feet) or Hexezeeche (witch sign).
Not too long ago, Dennis Boyer, Berks County author of Once Upon a Hex wrote to me and described the Hexafoos as follows:

"My primary pow wow teacher 'prescribed' hex signs, but did not paint them herself. She often referred to them as 'picture prayers.' Her method and concept were also present in a number of other Berks and Lehigh brauchers, mainly in a belt from Oley to Macungie, though I heard of a few others up in the Mahoning Valley.

Other terms that popped up were visual prayers, dream signs, wish symbols, and magic marks. I've been told of brauchers long ago that drew such symbols on the body of others and of one who had India ink tattoos in the palm of her hands. I had a dream of having such a tattoo on my left upper arm. Haven't moved on that yet. DB"

I refer to myself as a Hexologist, not a Hexenmeister, though there are areas the two have in common. For example, Hexologists won't use urine or other bodily fluids on their work as a Hexenmeister might do as a part of a magical practice. Instead, a Hexologist will let the paint do the talking. My knowledge of Hexology is derived from my birth and subsequent youth in a place called Berks County, Pennsylvania. In the 'native' dialect it is called "Barricks Kaundi." I am a Deitscher. My family came generations ago from Switzerland and Germany to the Oley Valley in Berks County and remains there still. We are Pennsylvania Dutch, Pennsilfaanisch Deitsch, Deitschers all…Hexology is in our blood.

If you have my cousin Don Yoder's 'coffee table' book

Hex Signs, Pennsylvania Dutch Barn Symbols and their Meaning, (E.P. Dutton, New York, 1989) and look at page 19 which shows the frequency of hex signs in the SE part of PA, right where the dots all converge and it gets all black…yeah, that's where I'm from.

'Natural Born Killers,' 2008 Hunter Yoder

I painted Hex signs on my father's barn in Richmond Township near Virginville when I was about 16 years old. He grumbled at the extra expense since the
I painted Hex signs on my father's barn in Richmond

Township near Virginville when I was about 16 years old. He grumbled at the extra expense since the 'job' was to just paint the whole barn one color, ha! But there they were actually inscribed into the wood and calling to me, the usual three on the front bay, and one on either end, but none on the back bank side—eight-pointed stars, with a radiating outer border.

I also grew up and went to school with the Claypoole family, whose dad Johnny, took up hex sign painting as taught by Johnny Ott of Lenhartsville, not too far down stream from us. I loved Ott's work. It still was pretty visible back then on the barns around the area. He was basically a commercial painter with a little something extra. The interior of the main dining room of the Lenhartsville hotel is the Sistine Chapel of PA Hexology. Ott free-form decorated all the walls. It's still there to visit. Lee Gandee, in his book Strange Experience, relates the following anecdote about Johnny Ott: A rain hex sign he painted was evidently left outside too long causing so much rain that the Delaware River flooded, causing 4 million dollars damage, a large sum back in the fifties. Just one example of the power generated by these painted prayers.
My family was Lutheran and was considered Fancy by our Plain Amish and Mennonite neighbors.
My family was Lutheran and was considered Fancy by our Plain Amish and Mennonite neighbors. The Amish and Mennonites always had the best land on the plain in Berks County. However, the tradition of painting the Hexafoos was never a 'Plain' one.

'Reyn til Runa, Sex Magic Hex' 2008, Hunter Yoder

Hexafoos can be separated into two general categories, six-pointed stars or Rosettes, and the eight-pointed earth stars, with the earth star being most commonly seen in Berks County.

The Rosette as an archetype is found throughout antiquity. It was embraced by the original Germanic Heathen tribes of Switzerland, where it was used as a talisman and painted on barns; a practice that jumped across the pond to Pennsylvania and is still in use today. According to Lee Gandee, six forms the most stable unbreakable configuration in the Universe (Strange Experience, Autobiography of a Hexenmeister, Prentice-Hall, 1971). In Yantra, an Indo-European symbological tradition, six is the union of the male and female forces, the male being the equilateral triangle pointing up and the female the equilateral triangle pointing down. Together they form an unbreakable bond.

The eight-pointed star or earth star, is a variant of the simple four-pointed star which points in the four compass directions. Eight is another archetypal number commonly associated with metaphysical cosmological models. The Berks County eight-pointed star in black and yellow is a condensed cosmology called a 'cosmogram.' It is both the sun and the earth, a source of energy and a sign of fertility and abundance. As we say in Deitsch, it's "gut glick" or good luck. The geometric shape it embodies is the square or diamond. These two together also create an unbreakable bond in the form of an eight-pointed star. We shall see later how this ties directly to the Elder Futhark's Ing rune.

There is, for me, a direct analogy between "hex sign painting" and growing plants, or perhaps more precisely planting seeds. They are both creative acts. When a seed is planted, all of the components of the mature plant are there in a very compact form. The results of the "planting" are not always known, and the conscious intent can be misleading. "Growth" sometimes occurs in such a way that is not anticipated. The subconscious mind needs only to be exposed to a conscious experience in order for it to manifest that experience's essence with a creative result. The ritualized intent of a Hexafoos is activated by some form of the irrational, which is slipped into the symbology, usually in the center. This can be achieved using disparate elements or some form of incompletion. It creates a question that needs answering. Examples of this in my own work might be the use of a black droplet instead of the traditional blue, or using a rosette with an eight-pointed star instead of repeating the star element. The human psyche will reject any form of incompletion and find a way to make it whole. This need or anxiety is the catalyst for connecting with our "Living Universe" which is inevitably paradoxical, and the results frequently a surprise.

I believe my focus as a Hexologist is also the primary focus of the Berks County farmer—fertility and weather control. The essence of Pennsylvania Deutsch magic is fecundity. As farmers we seek to increase our yield and protect our farms. Because of the simplicity and primitive nature of the intent, you could say that Witchcraft (Hexerei) and "Shamanism" are the main components of Hexology. Whether they are just different names for similar things, as has been suggested to me by Dennis Boyer when I raised this question with him, or different schools of thought—Berks County contains elements of both. The Hexerei came with the predominantly Germanic settlers as folk religion. The Appalachian Mountain Range that runs through its

Northern end was the conduit for the Shamanic element. Power plants used to induce hallucinations, rattle snakes, and power points in the blue rocks of the Deitsch Eck, or German Corner, attracted me in my young manhood. Events have occurred there that defy rational explanation.

'Schwarz Sonne Hex' 2008, hunter Yoder

My preoccupation with the connection between

Shamanism and Hexerei resolved itself in my discovery of the Northern Magical traditions of Galdr and Seidr. Galdr or spoken/sung magical spells seem to relate directly to our Deitsch Hexerei. It echoes Hexology with its use of sacred geometry and complimenting symbols to tune in the intent. The Icelandic tradition of Galdrastafir would be its Northern European cousin. Seidr is Northern European Heathen shamanism, indicated by its usage of power plants such as Bilsenkraut or Henbane (Hyoscyamus niger) and Amanita muscaria with a strong emphasis on intuition. These primitive magical practices are universal to all folk traditions.

My own evolution as a Hexologist has led me to include runic components in my work. As symbols and sets they have meshed wonderfully and the Heathen Germanic symbolism acts to 'power up' the Hexafoos. I have used the runic wheel as the border component, the outer circumference of a Hexafoos, and also in the center, usually in the form of a bindrune.
I use clockwise and especially counter-clockwise runic wheels and reverse runes as well where I see fit within the context of each Hexafoos. As a Deitscher, I do not claim to be an expert in the runes, but I intuitively relate to their flexibility, their mystery, and their ability to ground in natural materials, such as wood.
I use clockwise and especially counter-clockwise runic wheels and reverse runes as well where I see fit within the context of each Hexafoos. As a Deitscher, I do not claim to be an expert in the runes, but I intuitively relate

to their flexibility, their mystery, and their ability to ground in natural materials, such as wood.

The use of runes in the border has become my signature innovation. Traditionally, the border is very important and distinguishes one's signage from another. It also allows the artist to show off his personal skills. The border always depicts an expanded version of the core number of divisions. If the core star is an eight-pointer, the outer border is inevitably in some multiple of eight. As such, the runic wheel operates as a full set—a completion, a realization. This totality is the essence of Hex Magic, as it is with Rune Magic. Through this completeness the intention is realized. We live in a wanting, willful universe and we are the channels through which it manifests.

My first use of runes and bindrunes was in a piece called "Virginville Helm." It featured a "Helm of Awe" protective symbol in the center, and four runes at each of the four corners of the square it was painted in. It wasn't well received by a Deitsch Heathen group I was in contact with at the time as they weren't ready to make the connection between the Galdrastafir of the Icelandic tradition, and the Hexology of Berks County. I actually hid it away for a while, as I was still a novice in runic knowledge and unsure of the connections I made. I eventually found a Rune Magician who added to my knowledge and supported me in my work. Her name is Patricia Hall and I first met her at the very first Blót (Old Norse 'sacrifice') to Wotan of the Urglaawe or 'original faith' Heathen group in the SE Pennsylvania area. With her background in shamanism, and strong intuition, she was able to grasp my untraditional approach to Hexology, which in turn corroborated my own instincts.

'Flesh Blood and Cum' 2008, Hunter Yoder

As soon as I saw that "Helm of Awe," I knew it was

compatible with my own Berks County tradition. The Elder Futhark is composed of three sets of eight runes, a multiple of eight that lends itself to a wonderful outer border on a Berks County eight-pointed earth star. Using this as the border immediately suggested a center to interact with. The center is a place of convergence and lends itself to the placement of bindrunes, which are several runes in a composite form with a specific purpose.

My voyage of discovery had begun and the floodgates of creativity opened. I was next struck by a runic "Nine Worlds" configuration using Eihwaz as the vertical axis of the world tree and Gebo, the Meeting of Heaven and Earth, at the Four Directions in the horizontal plane, (see an example of this rune composite at http://home.earthlink.net/~9worlds/yggmaps.html) and its subsequent expanded form using nine Runes. Asgard is at the end of the top hook of the Eihwaz rune, then Ljossalfheim at the top point, Midgard is at the centre, where the Gebo rune crosses it. Svartalfheim is at the bottom point of the Eihwaz, and Hel is at its end. The Gebo rune is imagined to lie in a horizontal plane, with Midgard as its nexus. Eastward lies Jötunheim, to the South, Muspellheim, to the West, Vanaheim, and to the North, Niflheim.

'Nine Worlds Hex' 2008, Hunter Yoder

It accomplished what I had attempted earlier—providing a Runic Cosmology. It orients according to compass directions and even into more dimensions. This is very much in keeping with Hexology, since the Hexafoos are merely 'cosmograms,' or short forms of symbolic cosmologies. Using the Elder Futhark as outer border, I substituted my usual raindrops that spin in between the

eight rays of the star with eight of the nine "World Runes" and used the Gebo rune as the center, which fits it very well.
In subsequent work I oriented the Hexafoos using Ansuz as the top Rune and the rest accordingly with clockwise and counter-clockwise rotations. A note on the Deitsch usage of raindrops or 'yods': Along with the earth star or 'sun,' the raindrops promote fertility both in the physical plane and the spiritual. The droplets can be used as a cleansing purity, a gift from heaven…water. They are also used to symbolize sperm and blood, along with the multiple levels of meaning each of those have.

I carried this idea further when Patricia asked me to do a Hex sign using the "Reyn 'til Runa" (trans. 'seek the mysteries') bindrune of the Rune-Gild. This time instead of a nine worlds runic assignment in the droplets, I was instructed to use the rune of the opposed position within the droplet next to the outer Elder Futhark Runic wheel. For instance, use Uruz and Dagaz. If you write out the Elder Futhark…Fehu through Othila and then write it out in the opposite direction under each you will see the pairings…positional opposites. In the center, in an act of Deitsch "Sex Magic," I inserted the "Reyn 'til Runa" Bindrune within a black drop to 'activate' the Hexafoos. The effect was very visceral and erotic, simply through the use of symbols and runes. The goal was to 'impregnate' the Hexafoos with the high energy of a 'temporal mutual orgasm' and thus activate it into being.

In time, I became interested in the "Black Sun" mystical

symbol and thought it lent itself to Hexology. I wanted to use The Younger Futhark instead of the Elder because the number sixteen lends itself better to the Berks County Eight earth star. I wanted to make it run counter-clockwise because this also intuitively seemed natural. In the center, the sixteen 'rays' of the Black Sun emanate out to each of the sixteen runes. In the center is Odal (Othala). The eight counter-rotating droplets are the blood. And within the center is a stylized "GeilSkimmel," or Datura flower. This is a nod to Hexerei, as Datura is a symbolic power plant of intent. I also finally used the rune Sowilo as a bindrune, known as the "swastika" in Hexology. Its use as a bindrune was the attraction, and because of my clear intent, I no longer harbor any fear of using it. I depict it, and the runic wheel in which it is contained, counter-clockwise.

This led to a Rosette version of the Black Sun with six counter-spinning blood droplets and three more each inside of the other with a centered Ing rune. I have always responded most directly to the God Ing (Frey) as he represents the masculine fertility god of the Pennsilfaanisch Deitsch and of Hexology. The diamond shape is the giveaway. I have always painted Hexafoos on squares turned on end—diamonds. This orients the viewer to the four symbolic compass directions and sets the derivation of the eight-pointed star. This star represents fertility, abundance, and "gut glick" or good luck. It is the shining earth star of the farm, agriculture, and animal husbandry. These are all attributes of Ing, and I salute him at every blót I attend.

Most recently my rendering of the Black Sun and the subsequent "Black Sun, Blood, and Geilskimmel" Hexafoos have evolved into a state of "Black Sunshine." The outer Younger Futhark runic wheel is mirrored by an inner combination of eight runes forming a bindrune, which is centered within a single large blood droplet.

'Black Sunshine' 2009, Hunter Yoder

The bindrune combination can be determined by a blind pick of the runes. Eight runes are picked randomly, intuitively. This rejuvenates the process of making the Hexafoos. It is visually fresh because control has been relinquished in a very controlled way. It generates something unexpected or unknown. New pairings are created with the outer opposing Younger Sixteen Runic Wheel. Black sunshine emanates from this central composite outward to each of the sixteen Younger Runes which are now not only running counter-clockwise but have been reversed where appropriate, according to the spacing within the runic wheel caused by the reversal of flow, rather than to proper runic articulation.

The tradition of Hexology has never been Christianized, though many have tried to ascribe Christian symbology and meaning, so it need not be saved from the pile of Christian influences under which many of our other traditions have been buried.

'Flesh, Blood , and Cum," Detail, 2008,Hunter Yoder

Hexafoos images as well as Hexezeeche trace their origin back to the magico-religious practice of creating carvings on cliffs and paintings in caves depicting geometric symbols and animals. We can trace this tradition back at least 40,000 years to Cro-Magnon man in the area now known as Europe. Hexology continues in an unbroken chain from our Germanic tribal roots in Eurasia to our spiritual 'homeland' in Pennsylvania, where it thrives, not as a tourist attraction, but as a viable and evolving part of our Germanic culture. It is my intention not only to preserve this tradition, but to extend and expand it into the international magical art form it truly is, as part of the revitalization of our pre-Christian ways.

[About the word "Yod" – does it refer to the tenth letter of the Hebrew alphabet-the name of God? Or like in astrology-"the finger of god"? curious about the etymology~A] The usage of Yod is something I acquired in my youth in Berks County, I really am not sure of its traditional origin outside of Berks County. I remember it being used when referring to the raindrops on the hexafoos.

It's interesting because I know the term from studying the Kabbalistic Tree of Life when I was younger. Yod (the 10th letter of the Hebrew alphabet) is shaped like a raindrop.

Then later I learned of it through studying my astrological chart. A Yod is where three planets form an equilateral triangle and then activate a fourth meaning in their relationship "the finger of god." – divine intervention in your life. Coincidence?

Magic Plants Used Symbolically in Germanic Heathen Hexology, 2010

Originally published in "The Journal of Contemporary Heathen Thought, I"

I am frequently asked about the relationship between Hexology and the plants, or die blantz in Pennsylvania Deitsch. My approach to die blantz and their magic is similar to my approach to the runes, a learning experience. After spending time with herbalists and entheologists, and a bit here and there with the hoodoo root doctors, the plants breakdown in the following ways: as herbal remedies, as hallucinogens, and as powerful intentional agents. The latter is the subject of this article.

My introduction to Deitsch herbalism occurred around 1968 when I was apprenticed to a certain Bumbaugh, a name that even today makes the Xtian new age brauchers cringe. He was a crusty old guy with a penchant for making amorous overtures to the ladies who came into his establishment. Bumbaugh ran and lived in a kind of all purpose county store that was as dark and crusty as he was. Antiques, old books, herbs, and the occasional animal pelt were his stock in trade. All this thinly veiled what he really was and really knew. Bumbaugh knew die blantz.

One day my mother stopped in to checkout his antiques and when propositioned by ole Bumbaugh in return for a deal parlayed my apprenticeship with the old goat instead. My mother was well known amongst the younger witches in Kutztown PA Berks county and acknowledged as one of their own despite the fact that she taught Sunday school at the local Lutheran church. She and Bumbaugh understood each other.

Datura Stramonium

Bumbaugh's primary interest in the blantz was commercial and he started me out with collecting ginseng and goldenseal in various remote areas in Berks county to sell in his store. Despite his business approach, he had knowledge regarding the Deistch version of witchcraft known as Braucherei, a Christianized form of the original Hexerei. His nickname, Mountain Bummy, was a reference to a most well-known Braucher named Mountain Mary of Oley Valley, an especially haunted region in Berks county.

This was the area my ancestors came to from the Alsace-Lorraine district of Europe.

Ginseng especially caught my attention with its secretive ways. We found it in the nearby Blue Mountains. Its root is in the form of a man and it has a wildness that is commercially far more desirable then any cultivated variety. I also read about it in the early editions of Foxfire and was determined to cultivate it myself. Plants usually have their own ideas and this was my first test of wills with nonhuman consciousness

Blue Asherah, 2007

As I was walking the wood with Bumbaugh and opening to plants as conscious beings, I was also learning from

my friends the Claypoole family of Lenhartsville. The father, Johnny, was the unlikely heir apparent to the famous Hexologist Johnny Ott, who had, in addition to his well known hex signs, hotel/restaurant/bar in Lenhartsville called the Deitsch Eck Hotel. Claypoole was Irish Catholic from Philadelphia, but Hexology has a way of manifesting itself in unlikely ways and so it was that the torch was handed from one Johnny to another. I went to school with Mark and Kevin Claypoole. The family was large as Irish Catholic families can be. Johnny would put everybody to work for the various festivals. The biggest was the Kutztown folk Festival, now called the Pennsylvania German Folk Festival. Both Claypoole and Bumbaugh had prime locations at this lucrative venue. Bumbaugh was a well known fixture at the Saturday farmers' markets such as Renningers and had his used books, antiques, and herbs there. The festival created a special exhibit area for him trying to capture the inevitable authenticity the ole guy exuded. Johnny mostly did the summer festivals including the Philly Folk Festival and would go off in these events with his VW Microbus crammed with psychedelic hexes.

The third component here in my formation along with plants and hexes, is my introduction to art. My mother was a painter and I inevitably created most of her stretchers that I made from wood that floated downstream after the Spring floods on the Saucony creek that flowed though our farm. She took painting lessons in Allentown at the Baum School from a teacher named Martin Zippen, landscapes, still lives, portraits, that sort of thing. She took me along and I got a free evaluation from Martin who concluded that I had very little talent. My father viewed my painting career a different way. He gave me a brush, paint, and a forty foot oak ladder and told me to paint the barn.

Black Henbane

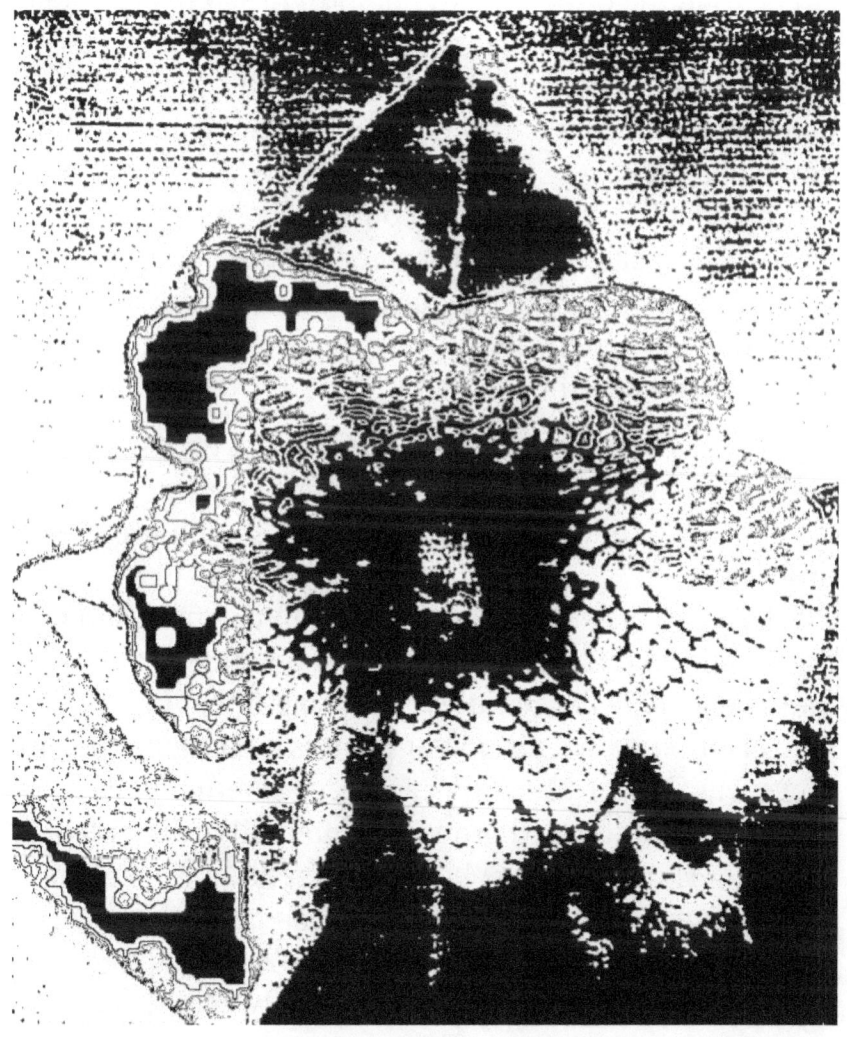

The PA German bank barns are famous as they are large. A highly evolved functional form of architecture, they featured a bank barn meaning that you can drive up to the second story via a banked ramp with corrals on either side with doors that rolled open on all sides. The doorways could be large as 12' by 40' in the back. In the front was the extended fore bay which was cantilevered out beyond the basic structure to provide a covered area to park implements tractor cars and tie up the animals, horses for shoeing, and hang the carcasses during butchering. This one also featured an attached milk house and granary. Painting one of these monstrosities was no small feat. But being continually in the 'scheisse haus' so to speak for one reason or another, usually involving coming home at cock's crow on school nights, there was little room for negotiation. I covered it with hexes…..and so it begins.

If you grow certain plants you realize that they have a will of their own and your idea of gardening might differ from theirs. Your idea of where things should grow will differ as well.

Plant energy is a very good one, positive connection to the living universe which is actually a lattice of interconnected energy fields. Speaking or having a conversation with a particular plant is a bit more specific however. The conversation can occur externally, the human as nurturer and grower or internally if the plant is ingested. If ingested, the human has relinquished some of his control and the conversation can be a test of wills as the nervous system is directly interfaced with the plant reality. Using a plant recreationally can be like taking one of those vacations where you get lost high in the mountains or desert and face a struggle for your life.

Belladonna

For me, of all the plants that have been used as herbal

remedies, as entheogens, or for intentions, the family Solanaceae stands out with datura, belladonna and henbane. These three plants talk the loudest and are the most willful. Some time the three uses are not so separate and it all blurs together depending on the individual 'user'

My experiences with datura, belladonna and henbane have been externally as a grower/nurturer, their unusual behavior and historical usage in witchcraft and most importantly their geometry has led me to use them in the Hexology.

The invoking of die blantz has been with man since our beginnings. It is a connection of consciousnesses that many of us have lost over millennium. Plants tend to take on a feminine nature, and as such are physical manifestations of the goddesses. In the ancient Mediterranean cultures, Asherah was a goddess as a tree, usually an almond. We see her frequently surrounded by rampant caprids which she feeds with her boughs. Eventually this imagery of goddess was stylized into a tree motif which eventually took form of the Menorah. As a fertility goddess, an asherah was frequently present in a stand of young trees, a grove. This took on a special meaning for me growing up in Berks County. In my travels "off road" I would come across such a grove, just off the flood plain on some nice bottom land that went wild. Under the trees in the grove, there was no underbrush, very clear and the rich soil was impressed with thousands of whitetail deer footprints. Obviously from the bark rubbings and such signs of activity, this was where they congregated for mating.

Black Sun Hex, 2008

Pa Deitsch lore speaks of The Elder or Sambucus canadensis, or as they say, Hollerbier after the goddess Frau Holle. The bush like tree is planted behind the house as a guardian, for she is a goddess of home and hearth as well as the goddess of the underworld. She is depicted as an old hag and her presence protects the house. She does this by grounding out negative energy and directing it underground. She prefers wet rich habitats and her roots reach down into the water table. Stone farmhouses in southeast Pennsylvania were always built on lower ground just off the flood plain locations so that the hand dug wells were not such an ordeal to create, and perfect for this guardian.

Male energies in magic plants exist as well. However maleness in a plant spirit is not quite the same as a male spirit of an animal. Common Mullein or Verbascum thapsus with his erect candle like flowering stalks is masculine in the sense that a lightning rod is masculine. Again in Deitsch lore, the candle of a common mullein is carried in the back pocket not to conduct but to prevent accidental lightning strikes.

Another not native to Pennsylvania but an interesting male energy is the Huachuma, or San Pedro cactus, Echinopsis pachanoi, or formerly, Trichocereus Pachanoi that is employed in High Andean Shamanism. This one is a tall erect cactus that is masculine in the sense of an old wise Grandfather. It is the 'cactus de cuatro vientos' the sacred cactus of the four winds, and it grows amazingly well in the Zaubereigartens of southeast Pennsylvania along with other South American power plants.

If you listen you will hear plants talk. One in particular that speaks loudly and clearly and can be extremely demanding is Valerian, or Valeriana officinalis. While buying herb seedlings at a farmers market, a robust valerian plant instructed me to, "pick me up and take me home!".....so I did and she has multiplied 100 fold for me. The children of this plant have not lost the willfulness of the 'mother'. More recently, one became unhappy that it was not first on the list to be watered and demanded attention. In fact, she screamed for attention…and got it. Plant spirit is often surprising. This particular willful prima donna is used often as a sedative and to ease nervousness and stress.

Plant spirits, facile as they are, also possess the ability to change sex. Arisaema triphyllum or Jack in the Pulpit is a very strange plant that I met very early on in childhood. Once wandering into a part of the woods I had never been to before I encountered "Jack" who promptly spoke to me and told me to "get out!" These come either male or female but if in the close proximity of another of the same sex can change the following year to an opposite one to insure success in fertilization. They do not have bulbs but 'corms' and the leaves are trifoliate which makes them useful in the Hexology as we use three because, as taught from antiquity, "three's the charm".

Most recently, I encountered "Jack" on the Hexenkopf, a strange piece of rock outcropping or the technical term is a mountain pillar in Northampton County, PA where my tribe, "der Stamm" was holding a Walburgisnacht ritual. This place historically was a place "Hexes" or witches would congregate in Colonial times in Pennsylvania. Not a part of the Appalachian Mountains which are nearby, it is a distortion in the time/space continuum. On this occasion after shepherding all but one of the tribe off the Hexenkopf and back to the safety of their cars, I returned for Patricia Hall, who had stayed behind to listen to the place. The walk back up off the road is a relatively short one, and one that I had made several times that day without incident since I was really the only one to know the way. Unexpectedly as I was returning for her, I became lost and knew that the place was playing tricks on me. It has the strange effect that nobody can hear your calls even if they are nearby. Such was the case with Patricia, who even saw me pass by but thought it was someone else and so did not call out to me. Knowing the Hexenkopf and its ways I used my mind and circled back onto her location at the rock altar. Upon our retreat from the mountain we encountered, "Jack". I was unhappy with the mountain for trying to take her from me, so I pulled Jack, a part of its consciousness, out of the ground to take home......Jack screamed and I involuntarily let go at first, but succeeded and stuck him in my pocket. Later we planted him in one of the gardens we keep.

Geilskimmel Fertility Hex

The turning point in my Hexology was my reintroduction to Datura Stramonium. This occurred in of all places, Brooklyn, NY. I knew her from my childhood. It is interesting that to children the names of plants are not important. Playing amongst them is the thing. This lady is infamous but hugely important in shamanism, and I was determined to find her again. As I wrote in my blog, "Frank Blank in Brooklyn:

"Red Hook, NYC's version of a Stalinist-Leninist State, or perhaps NYC's version of Mao's "Great Leap Forward" A grim reminder of what happens when Big Brother controls all aspects of its citizens lives. An example of what billions and billions of dollars achieves when flushed down the toilet, right you got it....a clogged sewage system. From the Projects to the Red Hook recreation area, to the razor wired pedestrian bridge over the BQE into the public school which sure looks like prison. You paid for it I paid for it, we all did......it might as well be a federal penitentiary, you get the unique view of the world through a high security fence. The occupants are....pretty vacant....all employed by the state...wards of the state, permanently damaged and in the business of self replication in a backdrop of a commercial warehouse zone with heavy trucks filled with hard toxic sewage, recycled paper and a pervasive odor of smoked fish/ a known carcinogen in the air. even in the new Brooklyn's spectacular real estate development miracle you can still get down to basics in a porto john in red Hook, where the homeless still can chill and shoot up in peace.....my kinda place. Be careful though, red Hook is the most police enforced zone in the 76th precincts' jurisdiction. They fund their personal retirements on the summons written here. Oh yeah this is where you go to take your drivers road test in Brooklyn. So amongst the garbage and deserted lots and places the park employees forgot to sanitize I found an old friend from my childhood......Datura Stramonium growing free and unknown to this mindless crowd. God bless the United State of my mind."

Her smell was her signature, not a rancid or funeral parlor smell as described in books, but an undeniable presence. I dug her up and took her home to my garden.....what a mistake.

I grew her successfully and indulged a bit in smoking her leaf with my Rabbi friend who lived next door. We both had unfortunate consequences with this adventure so the following year I was determined not to grow her again. This plant likes me and she came back on her own without me planting seeds and she has never left! In fact she has worked her way into my heart and into my art. Her five pointed pinwheel flower is a no brainer for the center of a Hexafoos. In the Deitsch dialect she is called Geilskimmel, which is a curious reference to horses. From my childhood on the farm, I remember that horse could become foundered if it ingested the datura, called "jimson weed". Her willfulness can only be experienced if you try to grow her. She will grow when and where she chooses. A force of this nature is useful in Hexology.

I have used her so often that she has been stylized into a symbol. As such I have integrated her into other more familiar aspects of Hexology, especially the raindrops. Rain drops are used traditionally just as that, both as water for the plants, the crop on the farm, and spiritually as a manifestation from above or in the Braucherei or Xtian context as a spiritual cleansing. I prefer to use used droplets in the context of Hexerei as sperm and blood. Coupled with the "Geilskimmel" I have created in effect the beginnings of a bindrune with the combination of nature spirit and traditional Hexology.

The third element is the rune or bindrune in the center of the hex to complete and seal the intent. Ingwaz works well with Lady Datura.

Black Sun Black Henbane, 2009

Once Datura Stramonium and I established our relationship, I was determined to find other plants specific to Hexerei. The Black Henbane, Hyoscyamus niger, also known as Niger Bilsenkraut became immediately apparent and I purchased the seeds from a French Canadian witch and grew her. True to form, she was very particular and would germinate but not grow to fruition as normal plants would. This one is trickier than and just as willful as her sister Datura. The flowers are striking. She has the usual inverted pentagram shaped flower configuration with a spooky dark veining on the petals, unique among all flowers to my current knowledge. We experienced success at last with this one at the Downingtown, PA Zaubereigarten which is Patricia Hall's place and has that gingerbread cottage in the middle of the Black Forest feel to it. So it was no big surprise the Niger Bilsenkraut would flourish there. What I could not grow, Patricia did. It liked her first, Hex that she is, and me next, male that I am. And so it goes with these deadly ladies.

This same season, the Belladonna Atropa seeds, earlier planted, flourished along with the Datura Stramonium under a bed of 12 foot sunflowers. This sunflower variety has significance to the Deitsch culture via the Chihuahua desert in northern Mexico. The Mexican government invited Canadian Mennonites to come to Mexico and settle a desolate, dead section in the state of Chihuahua, which was inhabited by the Tarahumara, an indigenous tribe whose ceremonial usage of a small native cactus, peyote was made famous by the French

author, Antonin Artaud's book, "The Peyote Dance".
The Mennonites transformed the Chihuahuan Desert they settled upon into a garden and exchanged seeds with the Tarahumara. These were the snow white seeded sunflowers under which the much darker Belladonna prospered.

Belladonna flowers also appear as an inverted pentagram along with Datura Stramonium and Black Henbane. So it is easy to see how these guys have been viewed as agents of the devil in the monotheistic religions. Dämmerschlaf or Twilight Sleep, was a well known combination of the Belladonna and the Opium Poppy, the effect was a dream-like waking state. This was prescribed by doctors in child birthing to deaden pain in Victorian England. The tropane alkaloid, scopolamine can be found in the honey of bees when they drink from the flower. Even the sting from a bee who has ingested the flower's nectar, can have a hallucinatory effect. Our experiences growing her have been a mixture of luck with an early success with her this season, and being tricked by her look a likes, namely pokeberry and nicotiana rustica. Just when we thought our consciousness had been lifted and the blinders pulled from our eyes with this one, she reverted to confusing us. So it's been joy mixed with confusion although we have enjoyed a very good season with her this year.

Belladonna Hex, 2009

These pentagrams or star like images are essentially feminine in nature. Feminine energy is an endless resource and only requires a directional impulse and a coupling. The
more intense the coupling the better the power the hex has. Usage of plants,
special plants in a stylized manner is just another way the Hexologist can tap into
the universe of feminine energy. And so I use Datura

Stramonium, Black Henbane, Belladonna. The willfulness of these plants can be used not by imposing the magician's will but by allowing their unpredictable nature to equal out the discordant psychic energies in a creative
natural way. This will always work in a positive way. The natural universe is
always seeking the most direct route to resolving dynamic energy inequalities.

As a Hexologist, I prefer to work with nature and let it decide. My job is only to pose the question, not impose my will. If the question is a good one, there will be an answer. The need will activate your subconscious mind

and what is sought is usually right in front of your eyes. Is it magic? It's Hexology.

The Reanimation of Germanic Tribalism in PA Deitsch Hexology, 2010

'Berks County Helm' Hunter Yoder

In the year 2007, I combined a traditional Pennsylvania German 'Barnstar' motif from northern Berks county with an Icelandic Galdrstave. Both worked on a framework of 'eight' radiating from a center. At that moment it became very clear that Hexology would never be the same again.

My personal story is not unlike many other personal tales of discovery of one's own tribal identity. However, the impact it would have on the greater Heathen community is unique and is the basis for this article. My background in hallucinogenics evolved into an interest in entheogens, Entheology, in the nineties and early two thousands, largely involved the usage of Salvia Divinorum, mescaline bearing cactus and Ayahuasca, a DMT concoction and Psilocybin mushrooms. However there were scores more plants that were used for thousands of years in highly evolved cultures throughout the world. One is hard pressed to find an ancient culture of merit that did not possess a tradition of entheogenic usage in a ceremonial context. At this time, shamanism is a word that is attached to many of these plant usages. Germanic witchcraft or Hexerei has a long history of plant usages and I became attracted to it via my lifelong experiences growing plants, which is the subject of another article or two. This combined with a lifelong obsession with Hexology became the basis for the realization that I did indeed have a tribal context in which to focus my creative energies.

In recent years, Hexology has been considered a dying art as was all of the Pennsylvania German (Dutch, Deutsch, Deitsch) lore, as reflected in the NY Times article on Johnny Claypoole's heir, his son, Eric . "For The Pennsylvania Dutch, A Long Tradition Fades". http://www.nytimes.com/2006/07/22

Simultaneously and quite independently, Folkish Germanic Heathenism was being born in Pennsylvania, and elsewhere. Rune magicians who had evolved into the Icelandic magical traditions were beginning to realize that the blood coursing through their veins was largely continental German and that their ancestors on this side of the pond had arrived, and lived first in Pennsylvania, before moving further west.

All things Pennsylvania German became the rage led by a seemingly rabid interest in 'new age' Braucherei which contained aspects of true folk magic along with a smothering overlay of Christian influence. The truer or 'mother' form, with no Christian overlay is Hexerei, a form practiced openly by only a few and without fanfare or a need to make a buck on it.

This awakening spawned scores of books on the subject of Pennsylvania German folk magic in its Christian form, Doctoral theses were published, and it became the 'belle de jour'.

Meanwhile, Hex signs had been largely dismissed as being, 'unmagical' and 'chust fer nice' The term Hexology is a relatively new one, being coined by Johnny Ott and Jacob Zook in the late nineteen forties, when the post war boom put America in automobiles and on roadtrips. Northern Berks County in PA became the ideal place to vacation by car. It included, Crystal Cave, Onyx Cave, Roadside America, Trexler Animal Preserve (where I used to feed my younger brothers the crackers meant for the wild animals), the Blue Rocks and many a natural wonder. It also included the Kutztown Folk Festival. A Festival devoted to PA

German culture. Quilts, funnel cake, pretzels, apple butter and hex signs were on display being created and sold as souvenirs.

The Hexes had to be portable, and unlike their ancestors, not attached to architectural structures. Johnny Ott painted them on circular masonite or plywood disks for sale. Jacob Zook had the designs silkscreened for a fraction of the price of the hand painted ones. And they are still very much in business…
http://www.hexsigns.com/

The old work still was visible on the most notable architectural structures in this largely rural farmland, the barns. The barns themselves were monuments to the ingenuity and craftsmanship of our Deutsch ancestry. The signs were the finishing touch and were usually embossed or inscribed into the wood. The work of Milton Hill was very visible and his work was on the barn I repainted in Richmond Township, near Virginville, PA. He was famous for his scallop work and adept use of color. "I like them loud," he would say of his choice of colors.

The awakening continued and cyber Heathenism hit and became especially strong starting in 2007. Pennsylvania German magic was polluted with outsiders with only an 'informational' connection to the area. Ancestral blood ties and cyber information, however powerful or accurate, cannot trump the experience of living in the area. There are just those little details that differentiate the real from memorex. I recall a yahoo list with a 'self-anointed' Hexenmeister who verified his PA German experience by accounting stories of eating funnel cake and being allowed to drink wine with meals as a child. Those of us on the list who were real 'Deitschers' knew immediately he was not one of us. I would make that criticism in general to cyber heathenism. If time is taken to recall life experience within a place, there is a strength of family and circumstance that is the source of one's Heathen self. It cannot be replaced and you cannot ever escape it and you cannot fake it.

Hexology was dismissed as 'unmagical'. However a towering classic, the true masterpiece on the subject of American Hexerei, was not so easily dismissed. Lee R Gandee's "Strange Experience, an Autobiography of a Hexenmeister" (1971) was not so easily dismissed nor were his exquisite Hexes which populated the cover and book. His references to Johnny Ott and his unique position that anybody can do it, changed everything for me personally and for everyone who has read the book or came in contact with Lee Gandee, most notably, Jack Montgomery who wrote his own homage to Gandee who was his teacher in, "American Shamans: Journeys with Traditional Healers".

Hunter Yoder after Lee R. Gandee's, "The Rain that refreshes the Soul"

That term, Shaman, again. When I questioned Berks County native and author, Dennis Boyer, about that term in conjunction with PA German Hexerei, he suggested that witchcraft and shamanism were the same. Dennis has an authenticity regarding Berks County lore that lent a great deal of weight to me personally. He remembered ten cent drafts of Schmidts' beer with kielbasa and Polish mustard, red beet eggs in a jar of vinegar on top of the bar at the Grand Central Hotel in Fleetwood, Pa.

The Hotel was open 24 hours to accommodate the three shifts of local factory workers. I had wooed many a lady with these delicacies in this traditionally Deitsch manner. This was a time when Fleetwood boasted Red Cheek Apple Juice, The Tannery, and where Fleetwood Cadillac interiors where originally created. All these, and other, medium industrial operations employed the Pa 'Deitschers' locally, right by the Reading railroad tracks.
Dennis characterizes himself on Facebook currently as being a "Shaman, Zen Mennonite". This sort of eclecticism which would have been cutting edge and 'cool' until recently seems to becoming increasingly irrelevant now. Both he and Montgomery mixed and matched magical traditions like discounted ladies fashions at a strip mall on the Lancaster Pike. Hell I have been just as guilty, most of us have. This criticism is not to say that they did not have expert knowledge far exceeding my own, just that they seemed to lack the focus necessary to really be a nut cracker and rescue the Germanic traditions in North America from any further obituaries in the NY Times. This singularity of focus was rapidly thinning the men from the boys. It was an article in issue four of Hex Magazine, by Galdragildi Rune school founder, Gandvaldr Bláskikkja called "Gandreidr, The Magic Ride" that warned of mixing Neo Shamanism and Germanic magic, that really finally made sense. Shamanism is not Germanic, period. No more Krauts in feathered head dress, if you please. The so called Indigenous Cultures are alien to those of Northern European lineage. The desire to live a life

within a tribal context, with a tribal identity had romanticized Indigenous magic and the juggernaut of Western secular culture had denied the existence of European tribalism. Meanwhile Western religious culture, led by the Catholic church, wrought such destruction on both sides of the pond. It had also removed the more ceremonial, esoteric elements from its services with Vatican II in the mid 1960's. There now was not as much Latin, not as much magic, in other words the good stuff. The Protestants had already removed these elements in varying degrees depending upon the variety and position in the hierarchy from high to low Protestantism. Recently I had the pleasure of meeting two Baptists who were going door to door to witness for their Lord. They were of Polish/German and Irish/German descent. I noted that it was not by chance that the three of us had met, and that blood is not only of importance in Christianity. Their view denied symbols of all kinds; the emphasis was on belief alone. When I suggested that the name Christ was itself a symbol, they had no reply. When I admitted to honoring the life-giving properties of the sun and that Aryan means 'sons of the sun' they replied that I was indulging in worshiping the creation and not the creator. They had a pretty strong grasp of the concept of animal sacrifice and the exchange of the sacrificed animal's blood for ceremonial intention, something that is done routinely at Germanic Heathen Blots. However I left my Baptist friends with an invitation to come together as blood, if they ever felt such a call. They closely examined my name, especially the first name, Hunter (no twelve apostles here) and left, puzzled.

With the decline of Christianity, those of European descent who already had strong doubts about monotheism naturally sought out a uniquely European pre-Christian identity. Our own strong tribal traditions were beginning to reawaken. Our own distinctly unique lineage contained the DNA for powerful zauber. This refreshingly focused viewpoint allowed me to attend to more pressing matters.

In 2009, I had organized a show entitled, "Deitsch Heathen Hexology" at Germ Bookstore/Gallery in Fishtown, Philadelphia. The Hexologists included, Patricia Hall, Swanhilde Ernst, Valufr Vaerelsson, and me. At least two of the contributors were Rune Magicians. Valufr headed the Wolfbund, the former Rune School, and was a well known scholar in the field of Icelandic magic. Patricia Hall was raised with Rune magic and Hexerei from childhood with an Austrian Grandfather, who schooled her in the runes, and a Polish gypsy grandmother who taught her straight-up magic. Swan had been painting magical Hexes for years and has a strong magical and art background, and I was just a simple Hexologist.

Patricia Hall, "Love in Marriage Hex"

Meanwhile, Germanic Heathenry in Pennsylvania had gotten ugly. Two camps had emerged. Urglaawe, a Deitsch name for 'original faith' was largely Universalist despite its rooting in Deitsch culture. It also embraced cyberism and alternative lifestyles. It allied itself with the neo-Christian witchcraft, known as new-age Braucherei. And an emphasis was put upon the dialect, Deitsch, which differs significantly from high German or Deutsch. The thing is there are a lot of Pennsylvanians who are German who not only do not consider themselves Deitsch, but actually are not.

So, the second movement was founded by Chris Loscar, who despite his relatively young age, was an old hand in the arena of German heathenry. Originally out of Pittsburgh, and a veteran of the US Army, Chris had a more Deutsch perspective then the Deitsch one. Chris also was a veteran of earlier failed Germanic heathen ground swells. In his own words, "I know what does not work." And so, a core group of Folkish Germanic Heathens, unhappy with the universalist and pro-Christian stance of Urglaawe, formed Der Heidevolksstamm. Der Stamm, as it is affectionately known is unapologetically folkish with a Germanic bent. It has since grown steadily with quality folk from all points Pennsylvanian. The purer, harder edged folkish aspects of continental European Heathenry coupled with the folk religious aspects of the Pennsylvania Germans was what we craved and so it came into being early 2009. Ultimately we wanted union with our European ancestors without the ancient imperialistic Mediterranean cultures' dilution. I found myself amongst individuals whose German ancestry had reached Pennsylvania more recently then my own and I found their more continental Germanic ways refreshing and lacking the incestuousness and narrow mindedness that characterizes most Deitsch-ers. With a name like Yoder, I can get away with telling it like it is.

Chris quickly introduced us to two other tribes working along similar 'folkish' ways. First was the Irminfolk, out

of New York. Again more recent European Blood, German and Polish. Prost!
The second was a tribe called The Wolves of Vinland. They were out of Virginia. We met these tribes at Sunnawendi 2009. We all sensed an affinity for things wild, strong, and relentless. We three were producers, contributors, and creators; all forces of nature. Our magical sources were different, from an Icelandic death's pallid countenance approach to life perpetuating frank sexuality, drawing inspiration from the German fertility gods and goddesses. And all three tribes shared a keen interest in Runology, which soon came to play a proliferating part in emerging hexology.

Matthias Waggener, "Wolf Hex"

Soon afterward, these three tribes formed the Confederacy of Folkish Heathens and the first PA Folkish Winternights Event was planned for October

2009 in Virginia. It was at a Hexology workshop at Winternights 2009 that the germ was planted in these three communities to produce Heathen Hex signs, with each newly emerging Hexologist adding their own unique perspective. Add to the mix, a few far flung Heathen friends, ex-Pennsylvanians and German, and the stew was simmering.

For decades, Hexology had languished in the hands of the Christians. The Mennonites and Amish, or plain Deitsch-ers, would not paint such pagan symbols anywhere. They knew these things had a potential that was distinctly not Christian. They would be found on the barns of the fancy Deitsch-er's, Lutherans, Dutch Reformed, other Protestants. The folk practitioners of the art were largely craftsman with an interest in pleasing a buying public. They would be commissioned to paint Hex signs with a Menorah, Lucky four leaf clovers, various birds as in the famous Distelfink or Gold Finch and so on. No one thought of using Runic symbology or bindrunes. The old traditional Hexes had come very close however. A form of Swastika or Fylfots was used commonly, and as these Hexes were usually a form of sun and used the geometry to imply motion or spinning, such usage was a natural. The older Hexes, were usually in the form of a rosette, which is a symbol used everywhere in antiquity. The rosette contains the sacred geometry of the Greeks and Egyptians, the six pointed star sacred to the Hebrews, and of more interest to the Germanic tribes, some of which may have originated in India. The Hindu yantra's (6 pointed star) unification of male and female forces in the universe is articulated in its geometry to form an unbreakable bond.

Brigitte Yoder, "Rossette"

Six is a very strong lattice, strong enough to base an entire universe upon. The most direct connection for the rosette to Berks County however comes from Switzerland. Swiss German immigrants brought it to America. Still in modern times, Hexology was considered to be dying a slow death and the hole was being dug for its inevitable demise. It had suffered from the same malaise that all those of European descent had and that would be a loss of direction and a loss of a self identity.

Hunter Yoder, "Black Sun Hex"

Most hexes are set within the bounds of a circle, overtly or covertly through the use of negative space. The circle is a universal abstract geometric form. The wheel revolutionized civilization as nothing has since until the advent of the Internet. The wheel has always been of special importance to the Germanic tribes. Their continual migration from north of the Black Sea into Europe and Asia required the cart. The wheel of our own Black Sun or Schwartz Sonne was found in jewelry worn by women of the Alemanni. It stylizes the juggernaut/wheel and one can sense the inevitable power of conquest these tribes had achieved in their movements throughout the world. To incorporate such power into a Hex would in effect be attaching jumper cables to this supposedly dying art. This was no menorah, no Christ's blood, no shamrock, no distelfink. The reanimation of the Heathen into the Hex had startling effects. Patricia Hall who had given me Runic instruction for my Hex work gradually took a greater interest, first assisting me in the actual painting, and finally creating her own works. Hers contained magical intention that mine lacked and soon I was the apprentice and she the teacher in Hexology. The results were Hexes that did not impose a will so much as conducting universal equalization of dynamic forces, usually involving copulation. In other words I guess you could call me a farm boy.

I had the technical ability and she the Rune magician's magical focus. Her work ended up on the cover of Ancestral folkways magazine and became the logo for my website at the time devoted to Hexology and magic plants, www.zaubereigarten.com.

Arrowyn Craban, cofounder and art director of Hex Magazine, had created graphically the quintessential

feeling of the Deitsch with just a bit of a harder edge that characterizes the Heathen. Her work in Hex resonated with me, confirming my suspicions that the reanimation of the Germanic tribes in North America would reflect the largely continental European population here rather than the smaller insular Deistch population. Her Scherenschnitte, or scissor cuts in the Muddersprachen,
were especially reminiscent of Fraktur work to me and are in fact a continuation of a tradition that started in Germany and Switzerland in the 1500's before jumping the pond to, you guessed it, Pennsylvania. We ended up working together on the cover of Hex's most recent offering. A Hex on the cover of Hex! She spoke about her work recently and said, "I started this long ago, before I ever knew that my ancestors had a tradition, but haven't done it in many, many years. I'll put up my old pieces and keep adding. I am really enjoying this as a creative outlet, it's so accessible. Very few supplies are needed and the possibilities are endless. "

Arrowyn Craban Lauer

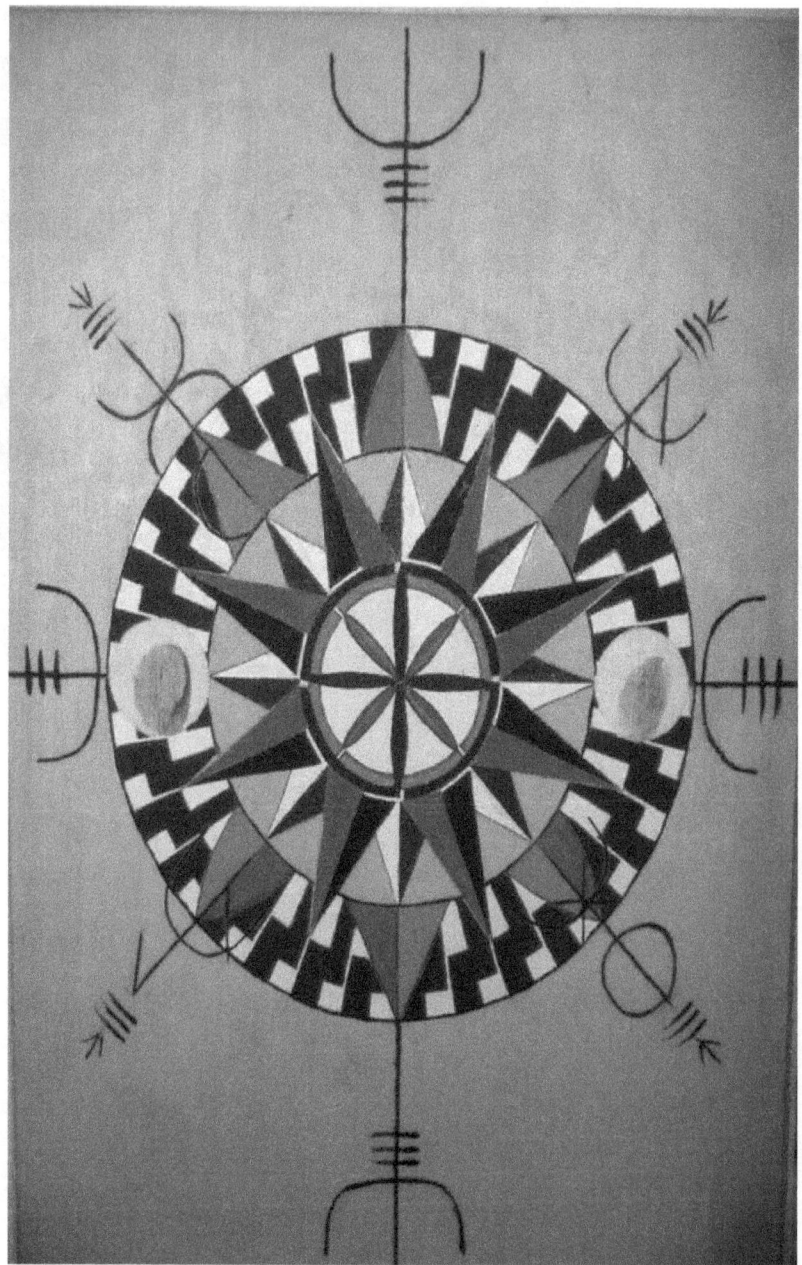

'Hamramr' Matthias Waggener

Matthias Waggener, of the Wolves of Vinland instantly knew what time it was at the Hexology Workshop at the Folkish Wintersnight in October of 2009. His work which is magically charged is guided by his participation in the Galdrigildi, a rune school. His incorporation of Runic intention into the Hex along with a universal division between the objective world and subjective self is textbook magic. He does some pretty good animals too, naturally a wolf, but he has done at least one excellent Distelfink. No love birds yet ladies. I have featured his work on the front page of the Yahoo group, The Backdoor Hexologist and his and many others' work can be found in the Backdoor's photo library.

Aaron Badger is another great Backdoor Hexologist participant. He hails from Rhode Island. Zaubereigarten went on the road and participated in a Vahallapalooza in Newport R.I. In 2009, where we picked up on The Badger. He is a New England based artist who practices a Saxon based version of Heathenry. He incorporates many of the runes from the Anglo Saxon Futhorc in his hexes, as well as medieval heraldic motifs and traditional Germanic imagery.

Aaron Badger

Rebecca Radcliff is a Berks County Heathen Hex and member of Der Stamm. She blew us away with a Hex that I had to coax her into displaying here. Becky managed to avoid all the constraints of being a Deitscher growing up in Moselem Springs just outside of Kutztown and is leading force in Paganism in SE Pennsylvania. She also has a green thumb. Her Hex, "Abysmal Awakening" has that 'Arise' thing going on. It reminded me of Von List's Feniks. She corrected my knowledge on Von List immediately and said, "The phoenix, right? I remember reading something where Von List referred to a fanisk as being the phoenix. That's pretty much where I was going with it. But this is taking place deep in the earth...the water drops and the background of the wolf are both in a deep, dark blue (why they look black in the pictures...I couldn't capture that blue). It was symbolic of where fire meets the waters deep in the earth for creation...more specifically re-creation, rising from the bones, the voices, on the grounds of our ancestors, continuity of tribe - one soul at a time. "

'Abysmal Awakening', Rebecca Radcliff

Krystal Anderson of the Wolves of Vinland and a

member of the Galdragildi, was eating hamburgers and fries during the Hexology workshop at Folkish Wintersnight 2009 last year but boy can she dish out the Helm of Awe and Runes within the Hex context. You can just tell she is having some fun with this folk tradition. She is from Minnesota and qualifies my response to her as being a Minnesota Viking by telling me it's by blood and not by professional sport. Krystal has the magic and her work is powerful in its simplicity and also in its depths, much like Krystal herself.

Krystal Anderson

Sarah Eppihimer, now in Alaska, alas we miss her, is doing some wonderful Hexes. Sarah and her husband Mark and I did the Hexenkopf proper justice on Walburgisnacht, 2008. They are Deitschers by blood so the Hexes come naturally. We always shared that warm fuzzy feeling that accompanies indulging in high caliber weaponry, corn liquor, hallucinogenic plants and running wild as the wolves of 'Deitschland' are want to do in the mountains. Sarah was born and raised in Boyertown, PA and keeps her ancestral traditions alive. She creates her hexes with intent and for a reason, or for a specific person or cause, e.g. Good Luck in an Irish-German Marriage or a new birth. Sarah uses traditional symbols and sometimes, Germanic accents such as runes. Every symbol she uses has significant spiritual meaning and every Hex comes painted straight from her heart.

Sarah Smith Eppihimer

My own daughters, I'm delighted to say have done some very impressive Hexes. Erika and Brigitte Yoder have been exposed to my Hexology since birth. Erika's Ostara Hex and her Smiley face Hex, knocked my socks off. She told me I needed to use more teenage symbolism and this was her answer to that!

Erika Yoder, "Teenage Symbolism Hex"

Brigitte has always had the 'wyrding' way, and when not doing Hexes she makes dolls out of last year's flower pods, this one is from Datura Stramonium, and is her Datura Fairy. When I have problems with rabbits which is frequently she is my intermediary in the animal world.

'Primordial' Mike Babbish, mein bruder in Der Stamm, is an intense young man who is steadily working his artistic way through the Runes, interpreting each one with rich symbolism. His latest Tiwaz incorporates two rosettes. Here is what he says about this work. "I included the two hex signs for several reasons. Hex signs, as you well know, were traditionally used as magic charms- often for the purpose of warding off wicked spirits and danger. The power of the two hex signs is demonstrated by the Fenrir wolf bound on the bottom of the picture. Further, All-Father Odin sacrificed an eye to the well of Mimir for a drink from the well of wisdom. The colors on the two rosettes represent the sun and the moon, and they contrast Odin's eyes - which were said to represent the sun and moon (the good eye being the sun and the sacrificed eye being the moon).

Michael Babbish, "Tiwaz Hex"

Lady Sunshine MoonRaven is a third degree High Priestess of

the Black Forest Clan, a euro-shamanic system that specializes in the practice of PowWow. The Clan has its roots in British and Germanic traditions and is dedicated to the training of Wiccan Clergy. Sunshine's roots are Pennsylvania German, or Pennsy Dutch as she calls it. Most of Sunshine's inspiration comes from her dreams. She has always believed that the simplest pieces of art whether in the form of music, words, drawings or paintings, are the most powerful expressions.. Once a 'piece makes itself known to her, she cannot ignore it. Her work has a freshness and spontaneity. If Henri Matisse were ever to have done a Hex, it might have looked something like this one.

Sunshine MoonRaven, "Dreamer"

These folks…and many more out there not represented here… are evolving Hexology as this is written. As with any creative endeavor the art and the artist 'true up'. Each has their own style. Elements may be similar but intent and the 'feeling' within each piece are unique to the artist. It is a beautiful thing.

Germanic Heathen Hexologists are creating Hexes with nine pointed stars, nine having a special significance in Heathenry as in the nine worlds, nine nights, and nine Noble Virtues. We all also use the eight, or earthstar, as in the division of the Elder Futhark into three groups of eight; the sixteen as the number of runes in the Younger Futhark; the eighteen as the number of runes in the Armanen Futhark and the number of rune poems; the twenty four as the number of runes in the Elder Futhark; and three which has many applications as in the three sisters at the Well of Wyrd.

Traditional Hexology embraces the number four which is the basic 'earthstar' indicating the four directions. Eight and sixteen as being multiples of the earthstar four, a kind of compass rose. Six as being the number of the Rossette and 'witchcraft' in general as in the dual meaning of Hex. Twelve goes as months of the year as in the solar Julian Calendar and the Christian twelve apostles. Occasionally five pointed stars are seen, but this is more of a secular decorative usage. Even numbers are preferred in Christianity, and monotheism in general the odd ones being of the devil, the exception would be three which is the number of the holy trinity and sacred in Judaism and Islam, and of course, the number one.

Rune schools routinely use the tally and count in determining runic charms. The runes of the Elder are assigned a numerical value, usually just the number they fall in the order, one through twenty four. An oppositional pairing, or combinations of two runes created by running a backwards order beneath the normal order and creating twenty four pairs. The sum of the numerical values of each pair will always add up to 25. Many other usages are well known, however the numerical assignment is a relatively simple one. This practice may or may not have been used by Rune Masters in antiquity. This practice is very similar to the ancient Mediterranean cultures usage of gematria, which is a Greek word but is especially a well known practice of the Hebrew mystics or Kabbalists as per the 'Tetragrammaton' whose gematric sum equals 26. Their usage and numerical assignment is far more sophisticated and there are at least three different gematric counts that go on simultaneously. Hebrew magic was held in the highest regard throughout Europe, even Iceland. The so called German "Sixth Book of Moses" in name pays tribute to the Hebrew magic but is a mere shadow of the original Pentateuch. The reference is worth noting however.

It's important to distinguish the difference between numbers and geometry which exists outside numerical description. All the fuss about the classic irrational numbers such as Pi, Phi and the square root of 2 are just imprecise numerical descriptions of basic geometrical relationships. Numbers are simply a form of language. Remember Algebra class?. Gematria, Runic or Kabbalistic, is a linear sequence that is arithmetically manipulated and interpreted. The ancestral magical alphabets, the Elder Rune set of 24 or the Hebrew set of 22, go both ways, numerical and lingual.

A geometric figure exists as structure, not as a description. It can function both metaphysically and architecturally. Things need to be built. This is what creation is all about. The thing itself exists in the present tense and as such has an instantaneousness that all things have. There is no need for a lengthy, linear description to sense its being. The life of an object exists independently from the creator. This is the great paradox. Thought processes are imprecise analogs compared to a fully articulated object, which stands alone untouched and physically unchanged. Go to any museum. Djuna Wojton, a local medicine woman and author, says I am channeling Pythagoras..ok she may be right.

The same is true of the use of color. Red is pagan/satanic in Christianity as well as a symbol for the blood of martyrs. People of red hair are considered to this day as being, 'trouble'. This is because red is the color of Donar and any reference to him is pagan and 'evil'. Black is another one. Christian 'white' magic opposes evil, or 'black' magic. The Heathen community has routinely embraced the colors black and red, seeing them as symbols of passion and power and not evil at all. Black, of course, can alternatively represent, 'nothing' and as such is a good place to start painting a Hex upon. It also is not a color, which takes it outside the realm of color symbolism. Mostly it is an instrument of 'will' or intent without the Christian colorization of good and evil.

Clearly we create our world by our ability to define its structure. This is primarily done with language; we define ourselves through lingual constructs. This is in direct contradiction to the rigidity of physicality. Each construct lasts as long as our ability to believe it does. Without our belief, there is absolutely nothing. The old adage "Watch what you wish for!" is reliable. You could say that existence is an interesting interactive experience. Our mind is the indefinable element in this interactive experience. With it we can do things impossible by scientific laws. We can solve any problem given only the facts in the matter, as fragmentary as they may seem. The only necessary ingredient is a strong belief or intuition; this is the muscle that needs to be exercised. Dreaming also plays a role in problem solving. The unforeseen is our partner in a card game holding cards we can only sense it has. Magic is a tool in this game to influence that whimsical 'hand of fate'. My way is as a Germanic Heathen Hexologist who has had the honor of casting my seed onto fertile minds. Now that's Zauberei! I would like to thank those who I have met on this well worn path and welcome those I have not yet met. Whether with love or hate, and very seldom with indifference, you may remember my name.

+x+

Hunter Yoder

June 2nd, 2010

Six Questions to Six Heathen Hexologists and their Six Hexes

Published originally in Hex Magazine, Fall & Winter 2011 : Issue 9

Questions by Hunter Yoder

Answers by Patricia Hall, Gloria Dillard Brown, Matthias Waggener, Sarah Elizabeth Smith Eppihimer, Amber Faith, and Jakob Brunner

The Questions:

1. What is your background and personal geography in relationship to Hexology ?

2. What magical significance if any do you attach to theses signs and their symbols?

3. Whose work has influenced your own?

4. What thoughts do you have regarding the use of the Runes, bindrunes, and other Germanic signs and symbols in Hexology?

5. Same question regarding Plants and Animals.

6. Anything else you would like to add?

The responses:

Patricia Hall

I was born and raised in Pennsylvania of Austrian, Bavarian, Prussian and Polish stock. The Pa German side of the family, the Fritz's, influenced the hex sign side of my work. The house was marked with a protecting rosette on the outside and had fraktur house blessings inside… The Austrian side of the family, the Reichert's brought Heathenry and the Runes into my life at an early age as well. Add a little Polish witchcraft to the mix from my grandmother…and stir.

I am of the belief that everything has its own energy, directed or undirected by human intervention. Directive intervention may be imbued in the piece by a skilled maker, or it may attributed by an observer of any level. I tend to work with intent. Each piece has layers to it just like the mind…some will see purely an aesthetically pleasing piece at the surface level, some will feel an emotional pull of some kind, some will feel the intent, some will have a high awareness of the intent, some will not only be aware but be able to use the intent and so on. But all will have the intent imprinted on their subconscious mind. So, I am very careful and tend to use positive imagery for my public work.

Well, as far as this kind of artwork, I can honestly say all of the artists in this article and as well as several outside of this article have had an effect on me. Whether they are just trying this kind of work for the first time or have been at it for a while, the more we all do and share the more we influence each other. Everyone finds their own style and voice. It is a beautiful thing. And I must give a special nod to the traditionalists like Claypoole, Ott, and of course Milton Hill for his exquisite scalloping. And to all those Germanic folk artists whose unsigned work I have seen, in books, in museums, on tablecloths, paintings and woodcuts. And also my Austrian grandfather, Josef Reichert, who started me on the runes as part of created pieces when I was a little girl. He was a carpenter who carved the Armanen runes into some of his creations. What we are all doing now is an evolution of an art form that started with our ancestors and our progress with it is meant as a tribute to them.

Runes are a way of life for me so I only have a few pieces that do not incorporate a rune or runes in some way. I use single runes or bindrunes for specific purposes such as Health or Love in Marriage. A bindrune is made up of multiple runes whose individual attributes are energetically bound together for a specific purpose or intent as set by the maker.

I also like to incorporate the use of writing in some pieces. Writing may be done using runes or fraktur. Fraktur is a Germanic script named because of its broken or fractured appearance. The piece below illustrates this as it incorporates specific runic energy (Ingwaz rune) along with the magic of the Sator-Rotas square written in both fraktur and runes. This magic square was a favorite of the Pennsylvania German Hexes (witches) and had several uses. These uses are written in fraktur around the frame of the piece. In English, beginning at the top and moving clockwise, the uses are:

To Prevent Bad Luck

To Extinguish a Fire

To Banish a Fever

To Break a Curse

Plants and animals are an integral part of folk art and of my life. Folk, or the people's art was done for decoration but also to keep in mind the things important to life and survival, plants for healing, crops and animals for nourishment and survival. All non-human life has a consciousness of its own in addition to any man-applied attributes and I use them to focus or strengthen intent. I have a piece based on a Polish tablecloth I once saw with two sets of out-facing roosters and one set of small in-facing birds. Roosters are for protection in the form of vigilance and the small birds represent love, friendship and loyalty.

What is interesting about any piece of art is that it is a construct shaped in unconsciousness and filled with energetic attributes and substance by consciousness. Everything carries signature energy and can be used to convey specific meanings that will resonate at some energetic level with an observer. Creation is life is creation.

'Deitsch Hexerei,' Patricia Hall

Gloria Brown Dillard

My entire life I have been interested in and fascinated by circular geometry. I remember getting my first spirograph toy as a child and spending countless hours with it. When I was in elementary school I would trace the mandalas out of my dad's yoga books. Even as an adult before I discovered hex work I would spend lots of time doing Spirographs and using it as a type of meditation. After I graduated high school and my university plans didn't go as anticipated, I went to technical school for computer drafting. To get my certification, I had to complete a hand drafting course and I loved it. The intricate perfection and the attention to detail was just ideal for me. So as I got older and more interested in my family history, I learned from my maternal grandmother that we were Pennsylvania Dutch. I thought that meant our ancestors were from Holland until I started doing some research of my own. I came across some information on barn hexes and immediately bought a book. Luckily I still had my drafting supplies and I started drawing hexes on paper and coloring them with colored pencils and things just went from there. So, although I am in Texas, I love the Pennsylvania Dutch art and feel deeply connected to it. Plus, Hexes from Texas has a ring to it!

I think the sacred geometry of the circle speaks for itself and is evident in all cultures. Hex symbols in particular I believe to be highly magically charged with the intention of the artist. For myself personally, it is a wonderful form of meditation and can be close to trance work.

In the beginning, I was most influenced by Ivan Hoyt (he wrote the first book I purchased), Waldzauberer, and Swanhild. Lately I find myself moving more in the direction of Hunter Yoder's, aka Frank Blank, work.

Almost every hex I do has at least one rune associated with it. I consider who the hex is for, what do they need? What intention do I want the hex to manifest? From there, a rune will usually present itself. As I work, sometimes the rune will change. Hex work is deeply meditative for me and I concentrate on the rune I'm using and often galdor as I work. There have been times when I have intended to use a rune for a particular piece, but as I have tried to really consider what the recipient of the hex needed in their lives, runes that I didn't initially intend seem to force themselves into my mind. I really believe the use of the runes massively strengthens the manifestation of the hex. This past Yule, I made my mother a hex to work the Banishment of Negative Influence in the Home. She had been in a terrible relationship with an abusive sub-human for 15 years...I gifted her the hex, and by February her life had changed and she is now happily pursuing divorce.

For the most part, all of my hexes so far have revolved around runic energy and elementals such as Earth, Fire, the Sun, Water, the Moon, etc.

Gloria Brown Dillard

Matthias Waggener

I guess like most people practicing Hexology as a cultural expression, my background and link to the tradition stems from pedigree. Waggeners first came to Vinland at the beginning of the 17th century, and actually lived only a few hours from my present location of Lynchburg, Virginia. The name originates in Wageningen, Holland, and no doubt the family brought with it the knowledge of these mysterious barn paintings.

Although art and craftsmanship were highly valued and

encouraged as I was growing up, my first encounter with Dutch mysticism was through a friend of the family during our time as Mennonites in Wyoming. She would relate her Hutterite mother's "superstitions" and could oftentimes be heard speaking for hours in Deitsch- obviously, however, the Mennonite tradition was not my ultimate calling in life, and my next experience with Germanic occult practice came through the runes.

The runes turned into my first real esoteric pursuit. After years of working with them, as well as the creation of a great deal of art separate from any spiritual connection, I was privileged to meet the one and only Hunter Yoder, and was immediately intrigued not only by the beauty of his work, but also the complexity of the ideas behind them, a classic Germanic technique. I began asking questions and loving the answers, and have been working on developing myself through my work ever since.

In my opinion, magic is synonymous with intent. Intent is the seed of creation within the hexologist/magicians mind, signifying the willful mind's reaction to need, forming and directing that energy into a physical manifestation that is living; born of one's will and holding the prerequisite properties to take part in the creation of reality.

This requires a great deal of mental and physical focus, achieved time after time as I return to the original state of mind that was created during the works conception, and is held for each session until the work is done. On average, a piece will take me anywhere from 60 to 100 hours from start to finish, and generally consists of 3 to 4 layers of paint. It is that sustained and revisited mindset that is projected into the work, and every angle, numerical significance, pigment, medium, symbol and locale is a different representation of the initial intent. The resulting display is one of layered will, that will no doubt affect those who become aware of its existence, ingraining itself permanently into their consciousness.

As far as influences go, there is Hunter Yoder and Patricia Hall. I spent most of my first year studying their work and reading. I enjoyed their approach a great deal- I like to push the limits in everything I do, and feel like a found a real kindred spirit in Hunter. Their style is unique, while at the same time deeply immersed in traditional hexology at its core, making it a perfect touchstone with the past as well as an inspiration for innovation. There are also a large number of amazing Hexologists that frequent "the Backdoor Hexologist," a list which any in the know should be aware of already.

The use of symbols, runes, etc. within a hex are just further tools to enact different aspects and specifications , as well as create ideological relationships among separate expressions. I view a hex much like a "kenning," which Hollander explains as: "…a metaphorical expression that disguises its precise meaning until, through longer acquaintance, you arrive at the deeper insight it provides." As with hexcraft, you have a product that requires deep understanding and knowledge to "de-code", and the adding of runic symbols etc. allows them to become much more encompassing, as well as being more deeply layered and therefore more "hidden" and effective.

Plants and animals have always been a staple of traditional hexology. From the distelfink to the horse, oak and tulip, our ancestors attached deep significance to all living things in both their artwork and spiritual lives.. This makes them a sort of language of their own, in which the artist can speak to the perceiver. I like to use them in a classical fashion to pay homage to the style my ancestors used, that truly encapsulates the beauty that hexcraft can create.

Matthias Waggener, True Love Birds Hex, 2011

Sarah Elizabeth Smith Eppihimer

I grew up in a Pa German town called Boyertown, and am of German, Swiss, and Polish descent. Along with my family's heirlooms and hand-me-downs this is where I was first introduced to the Hexes and Pa Deitsch Fraktur. To this day Hex Sign's are still found displayed on barns and homes in the surrounding area.

After I started gaining sincere interest in the magick behind Hexology, I began creating my own hex signs about 5 years ago. As the years have gone by I've seemed to develop my own style and particular accents, along with a better learned magical approach.

Typically, the significance of my signs may be as simple as good luck, or spiritual blessings or protection, but most of my work is done with a specific person or charm in mind. Each one has been personally made with a specific purpose.

A lot of my stylistic influence comes from some of the more well know artists in the area, Ivan E. Hoyt, and Jacob Zook, seeing as many of their works are more popular and were seen throughout my childhood. But almost immediately after I began designing my own signs I started to incorporate symbols from my own spiritual background, i.e. Runes.
Soon after, I met Hunter Yoder, and realized that there was a sort of resurgence of our Folk Art. As well as the

traditional artists, Hunter has been an immense influence to me, especially with his rune work.

I think that the use of runes and bindrunes bring a far more spiritual and personal meaning to the signs for me. Even though many of the symbols used in Hexology are ancient symbols i.e. the rosette, the use of runes empowers and connects all the symbols together to possess even more spiritual energy, and reconnects them to even older traditions and/or our ancestors.

I believe that the use of plants and animals in Hexology is completely natural. If I were to make a Hex for my garden I would incorporate symbols for plants or leaves and probably use part of a plant/flower for the paint itself. And when I build my chicken coop you better believe I will have a Hex on the front with a big ol' rooster on it!

I currently live in Bear Valley, Alaska and continue to design and carry on the traditions of my German ancestors, whether it is painting, crocheting, or making homemade spaetzle in my cabin in the woods with my wonderful husband!

Luck, Love, and Prosperity, Sarah Elizabeth Smith Eppihimer

Amber Faith

I was raised in a sleepy historic Ohio River town in Southern Indiana, founded in 1803. There was a dominant German-speaking population spread over four southern counties; like my mother and aunt, I was immersed from birth in a syncretic Antebellum Mason-Dixon Line-meets-Pfalz und Trier gestalt. There were hex signs on a few barns and houses and hex embroidery patterns for sale in the country stores. Most of the nearby German farming towns were founded by 1800s transplants from Pennsylvania. The Amish and Mennonites were farm neighbors also; but, they didn't like Hex signs.

German was a second language in Indiana until World War I and it could still be heard from St Meinrad to Loogootee and Darmstadt Indiana during the 1970s and '80s. As an only child in a multi-generational family of historians, artists and antique collectors, I learned many Pennsylvania Hex signs' meanings and the certainty that authentic German use of plant foods was "body medicine" -- from homebaked rye breads, home-processed turnip kraut "mit Kümmel" to the varied uses of hops, mint and camomile. We baked Springerle and Zimtsterne cookies, could sound-out Fraktur script, attended annual Germania Mannerchor urban fall festivals and rode our horses in the Bierstube and Ocktoberfest of many tiny rural towns.

My maternal grandfather was of primarily Lippe Detmold-Teutoburger Wald lineage. My known maternal line of mothers descend from a 'Maria Margarethe ?" a Pfalz-Bavarian-Swiss girl who married another Pfalz German-Swiss lad (JohannesTroxell) in 1700s Pennsylvania. Between endless genealogy and getting that mtDNA test, I may find "my source."

My families proudly descend from concentrated German heritage, and old French, Scottish, English, Irish and pre-Roman Welsh bloodlines. For six years, I lived in Wiltshire UK and Wales, and traveled in Germany with my then young-son, Siegfried.

Runes and our dynamic herzlichen Hex designs that flow from genetic memory are linked. The runes inform and mirror absolutely on chthonic levels. Their use and play within German half-timbered architecture, door frames and older Hex sign art -- and the new generation of Tru Hexology -- reveal the primary shamanic sensibility of "Seeing patterns" in order to work spiritually between the worlds effectively.

Since the 1960s, I've purposefully used runes in ancestral iconic paintings, drawings and fiberarts. From 1981 through 2003, I designed packaging, named and created botanical products for the once-famous AIRS Incense, a California company I co-created in 1981. During the early days of AIRS incense popularity, I was the first American Art Director to include Magickal Guides on the back of each fragrance label, including the runes, meaning and Old Gods & Goddesses associated with that particular botanical. In my own way, I was intentionally creating in order to honour our Ancestral Gods and heritage. Back in the 1980s, when someone would send AIRS corporate offices photos of their new tattoos based upon my runic and mythic illustrations ... I smiled. Something in them had resonated and responded to those little encrypted blessings. Well-crafted Hex signs work in a similar way. People see them and wish to have one on their wall or house for unknown reasons. It's what we do.

Regarding use of magical and meaningful symbols in art: Gustav Klimt, the Celts and Picts, Carl Larsson, Robert Graves, Carn Euny and the megalithic cultures of Britain and Europe; W.B. Yeats, Leah Bodine Drake, Mary Webb; the entire Arts & Crafts Movement, Edred Thorsson; European prehistoric textile arts and embroidery and worldwide tribal tattoos.
As well -- Tibetan thangkas, ancient Hindu-Vedic iconography; Sumi-e & haiku; Saami and Sarmatian artifacts; the Mousterians, Magdalenians, Beaker Cultures, Hallstatt I & II, Solutreans and countless Danish shell middens.

(Hexes) can be uplifting, protective and very powerful, when created intentionally.
There may be moral drawbacks for Hexology fans with a need to 'sanitize' the early bindrunes. The runes, in my

opinion and experience, are legacies -- portals to Knowing. Sex. Blood. Birth. Death. Transformation. Voluspa said it all. Take them all the way or leave them by the trailside.

If Asatru/Heathen artwork and Hex work is new for an artist, my advice is Keep It Simple, Sister. The Nine Noble Virtues run parallel to the Scout Oath & Law. With those Virtues in mind before employing runes, bindrunes or untried Norse/Germanic themes in your Hex signs or project, you shall then be prepared for something lovely and paranormal to occur.

Discard coloring book ideas about runes, symbols and "cool Viking stuff." Instead, establish a personal relationship with the runes' compelling symbol-set forces. Bindrunes for protection and Vanic blessings, in adept hands, are alive and watchful. War-fetters, however, are another subject for another time. Inform your runework through living boldly, loving fearlessly and possessing Ernsthaft with Old Earth and Vorfahren values. Study the art of our Urnfield/Hallstatt/Solutrean/Nordic forebears for an hour and then wander around the garden or countryside awhile. Drink a horn of pure water. Make some wild love. Ride your horse or that Harley. Then, come back to the kitchen table and pour an inspired Hex sign out. It WILL work.

My protective Algiz-Hagal-Othala hex for the homestead ... painted on the tool shed, Amber Faith

In my own artwork and volva practices, essence-images of certain animals and plants of power transmit a message when used in Hexology. Healing herbs and certain entheogens are inhabited by challenging spirits (Landvaettir, 'kami,' devas etc) who have served

Northern Volk and Völur since prehistoric times. Psilocybe semilanceata and Amanita muscaria are described in many early European traditions. Using them in Hex signs may be a way of directing their etheric Landvaettir zest without running afoul of today's legal system.

Animal spirit companions, helpers or guiding totemic animals may speak to their Volk through Hex and rune art. In my work, I often find pairs or groups of totemic animal and plants demanding to "be" with each other in a painting or Hex sign. Seeing the pattern and integrating the elements with line, colour and emotion -- suddenly, there's a result. It's Hex.

Once again, the heathen artist appears as seer, shaman and mirror-holder.

Jakob Brunner

As a child I grew up in the Lehigh Valley and Northampton Counties in Pennsylvania. I was always exposed to my German and Swiss heritage which is my Mother's side of the family who came from Philadelphia. We must have always had a hex sign around my great grandfather Stewart Brunner's house, most likely a Zook. I remember buying Zook's with him and then watching him hang it on the shed which was more like a small barn. Since Berks county was so close it was common to get exposed to hexes there but I was further introduced to Scandinavian and Germanic Folk traditions and magic around the age of 18. It all came back together after moving back to Philadelphia in 2003 where I reconnected to the history of my ancestors in Philadelphia's Fishtown, and Port Richmond sections, while making trips to Bridesburg, Mayfair and Torresdale.

Of course art is magic if it is used as a tool as such and hex signs are a great Germanic folk art tradition that one can learn to use to help guide our intentions. Now my connection with the hexes came naturally, not only growing up in Pennsylvania and knowing a bit about them but also through blood in family heritage.

Personally I like traditional hexes the most but I am always a guy that goes right to 18^{thth} century traditions out of a personal historical interest. I find I get ideas from visiting the Pennsylvania German room of the Philadelphia Museum of art, but any one of the many heritage or art museums in Pennsylvania might have good ideas for hexes. Through Hunter Yoder & Patricia Hall I was introduced to Lee Gandee and I did woodcut studies of some of his hexes. Hunter and Pat took everything up a notch for me and reconnected all the information I had collected over the years bringing three points in one, my childhood, teenage years with the current moment. I started making the hexes under the name "Jakob Brunner" which it taking two names from my mothers side of the family, her Polish maiden name of "Jakubowski" and the old Swiss German maiden name of my grandmother "Brunner". There is also a German side of the family on my grandmother's side whose name was "Speier" (quite an odd spelling of the name). and 19

Runes, bindrunes, and other Germanic signs are an interesting hybrid that was also introduced to me by Hunter and Pat. I find this very interesting because it is rediscovering something in Germanic Heathenism that has been somewhat forgotten or lost for some people due to the fact that the bulk of the Heathen community seems to focus on Scandinavian aspects. I think it is nice that these aspects of Germanic Heathenism are brought back and using them in the hex signs seems to make them even more powerful.

Well Plants and Animals are always a classic traditional use in hex signs but of course again Hunter Yoder brings this up a notch.

I am very impressed with the current show at the Hex Factory, located in Kensington in Philadelphia (2080 East Cumberland). Kensington once had a large German community so it is nice that this culture is brought back into the neighborhood in a new form.

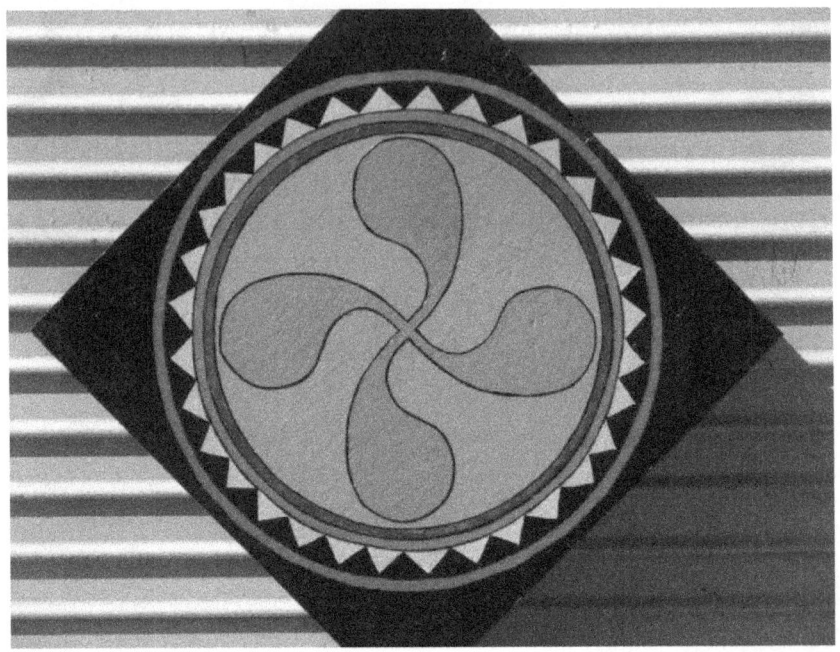

Jakob Brunner

Interviews

Hunter Yoder Interview with Valulfr Vaerulsson, 2008

Valulfr: Do you consider yourself a Hexologist or Hexmeister, and what is the difference?

Hunter: I would be the Hexologist, a 'Sign Painter'. The term originates in Berks County, Pennsylvania and is attributed to the Johnny Ott/Jakob Zook creative partnership that got the ball rolling. In the late 1940's they invented hex sign painting as we know it today. This would include the term, "Hexology". Zook came out with a book entitled, "Hex No!" back in the sixties, and I had a look at an early age. The color of the book was blood red, Johnny Ott was described in it as a Hexologist. This is the same Johnny Ott that Lee R. Gandee refers to in his masterpiece, "Strange Experience, Autobiography of a Hexenmeister". I would like to say to my Hexenmeister Bruders (tongue in cheek)that such a certification is a certification where no certification is necessary. Perhaps Hexenmeister is best used in the past tense, as for example Lee R. Gandee was a Hexenmeister, (also a Meister Hexologist). The idea of someone referring to him or herself as a Hexenmeister is hilarious. The old idea of a Hexenmeister doing battle with the dark Zauberer is xtian duality, good and evil, and no longer pertinent to Deitsch Heathenism which rejects the ancient imperialistic monotheistic middle eastern cultures.

Valulfr: When did you learn this craft and who from?

Hunter: I am a self taught artist, but as I mentioned

many times I grew up and went to school with the Claypoole clan. Their father , Johnny Claypoole, was the leading Hexologist of the times and visiting them and meeting Johnny and seeing his work was definitely an influence. I also painted the Hex signs on my Father's barn in Richmond Township, Berks County near Virginville, PA and that is where I came face to face with the Berks County eight pointed star. Another large influence was my 'apprenticeship' with a certain Bumbaugh, the owner of numerous used bookstores where he would sleep in the backroom on a dirty cot with all sorts of herbs hanging on clotheslines. Some of my xtian Schweschders in Berks County cringe at the name, LOL, but he taught me herbalism back in the late sixties early seventies. I have a picture of the self-styled,

"Mountain Bummy" on the Backdoor Hexologist list. He would collect Golden seal and Gingseng for money as well as animal pelts. He alternated between Niantic and Kutztown, and was fixture at the Saturday market auctions, antiques and produce, such as Renningers. I have fondly called him Braucherei's 'Fallen Angel'. I never separated my interest in magical plants from the Hexology. The geometry of plant growth is known as Phyllotaxis and is concerned with growth spirals. In classical geometry, Phi is the irrational ratio which best describes growth. The Hexology is an analogue or kenning for plant growth, life, abundance, fortune and love, or as we say in Deitsch, 'gut glick'

Valulfr: What is your heritage and when did your ancestors arrive in this
country?

Hunter: My ancestry has never been an issue, to me, the last name Yoder is Swiss German after a certain St Joder or Theodore who tricked the Devil into doing an impossible task for him in exchange for a soul, presumably his soul, LOL. The task was to take a huge bronze bell up to a remote village in the Swiss Alps before dawn or 'Cock's Crow'. The devil performed the task but St Joder had his influence on a certain rooster who crowed before dawn. My own particular line arrived in the Oley Valley prior to 1750 and the family remains in Berks County still. The name is usually associated with the Anabaptists but my Folk were Lutheran.

Valulfr: We read the term "painted prayer" when referring to the Hex sign,

which obviously denotes a Christian mind-set; how do

you see it?

Hunter: Obviously the xtian influence is there in that term, Painted Intention, Painted Charm, also work. Gandee uses that term in his book, and Dennis Boyer, a Berks County author also uses that terminology.

Valulfr: The term "Hexefuus", or "Hexefoos", used to describe the
Hex-sign. Obviously these are Deitsch terms; what is their origin and
 meaning?

Hunter: Well, Hexefuus and Hexefoos are variations of the same thing. Hex is Deitsch and Deutsch for 'Witch' and foos or fuus is 'feet' The idea was that the hex signs or hexezeeche, were footprints of Germanic witchcraft and charged with an intent accordingly, usually as protection or for favorable weather in the various levels of meaning weather implies. Hexefuus were always on the barns of the 'Fancy Deitsch' in Berks County. Barns were subject to fire due to lightning strikes, or by spontaneous combustion usually due to gasses given off by fresh hay. And then down below on the Swiss Bank Barn design were the cattle which were subject to the various misfortunes of disease, etc. Therefore, these

'Hexefuus' were employed to keep things going in the positive direction. Not only were they painted into the barn sidings, they were also scribed, and appear as reliefs up close.

Valulfr:
You are the nephew of the author Don Yoder right?
How does your
opinion of the Hex tradition differ from his?

Hunter: I met Dr Don Yoder in Kutztown at an event of the Pennsylvania German Society, http://www.pgs.org/ and introduced myself, he called me cousin, our exact blood relationship was never determined. The Yoders have been a prolific bunch. His line is out of Schuylkill County, which we 'Barricks Kaundi' boys used to call the 'otherside' being that it is on the other side of the Appalachian Mt ridge from Berks County. Dr Don Yoder is the grand old 'meister' of Deitsch Kultur, I'm just some wild son of a bitch who escaped the farm but never forgot where I came from. He has written many books on the subject and introduced me to the term, 'folk religion' which allowed aspects of heathenism to remain alive and well within the larger established xtian framework. Pennsylvania however was originally the place where many very unconventional xtian groups came to upon William Penn's invitation.

Valulfr: As with any traditional belief system, the philosophies behind them
change and evolve over time and regional stresses, how have the Pennsylvania Deitsch beliefs changed and adapted to the post-modern world we live in today.

Hunter: Well its funny you should bring that up, because it is a subject I personally find amusing. A couple years ago I contacted Ivan Hoyt, a Meister Hexologist, probably the leading one today (he doesn't call himself a Meister though, I do). When I introduce myself and they come to know my background, they have no choice but talk to me. Anyway, when I asked Ivan about the intention of numerology in his work. He dismissed it. This is old school Deitsch mentality where the idea that this 'stuff' might be magical was considered to be bad for the devout xtian tourist trade, LOL. This year reading some of the press coming out of the annual Kutztown PA German Festival, the old Kutztown Folk Festival, I'm seeing ole Ivan in full bloom, praising the magical tradition and not at all in denial. The whole Deitsch mindset has finally caught up with the new tolerance in our western culture towards the 'magische' as a capitalistic bonanza, a selling point. However, in

Kutztown, I know for a fact that my xtian hex schweschders have faced concern by the establishment for being witches. So it is a very conservative community which explains my exile to the more tolerant urban environs of NYC and Philadelphia.

Valulfr: What evidence is there for a "shamanic" tradition among our
Deitsch ancestors here in this country?

Hunter: I don't pretend to speak for the Deitsch community as a whole and I am not a scholar or a student of the past, I just recognize the fact that I am one by blood and experience. Shamanische is a very favorite topic to me. Shamanism is something that will cross all traditions, religions, and geographical locales. My experience with it is based upon my knowledge of plants and the specifically 'plant teachers'. The other ingredient is the Mountains, the Blue Mountains of PA, the Appalachian Mountains, that run from Maine to Georgia and with them the power of the irrational. Rocks are conductors for electronic magnetic energy that pulses just prior to dawn and again at sunset. My Deitsch teacher in the Shamanische would be Thomas Luckenbill who unfortunately is no longer with us in the physical plane. Luckenbill is an old Deitsch name, where he picked it up, I don't really know, but he had the whole package intact, every single thing I use today was from my time with Meister Luckenbill, this includes weather control, psychic transport, electric fur, sun worship, fire worship, and the power of the triangle and its three dimensional forms. A scholarly approach to Deitsch Shamanische would come from Dennis Boyer, a well known Berks County author, another one I contacted and had no choice but to discuss 'Barricks Kaundi Shamanische'. His view was that shamanism was just another word for Hexerei or witchcraft. His view may have evolved since then, but it isn't a view I share. I feel strongly that Deitsch Kultur has the Galdr in its spoken spellverk, aspects of Hexology, herbalism, and the Seidhr, my preference, in the more intuitive aspects of Hexerei, weather control, fore seeing, usage of plant teachers, in our tradition this would be Geilskimmel, or Datura, and the Niger Bilsenkraut or Black Henbane. These things I learned as I was well down the road towards High Andean Shamanism which came to an abrupt halt when I came to realize that the North American center for High Andean Shamanism was in the Appalachian Mountains near Roanoke Virginia! Well to make a long story short I flew into a rage, the idea that this tradition was encroaching into my Mountains was intolerable and I received instruction from my Plant Teacher to return to Berks County, my tradition in the shamanische was alive and well there, and so it is.......

Valulfr: How do you view the relatively recent resurgence of European heathenism? How does this relate to the Deitsch traditions and your role in it?

Hunter: As a builder, special care must be given to a house's foundation, xtianity was built upon a foundation of lies, my guess was that it happened at Nicea, the origins of the Nicean creed, although who knows. My Rabbi friend, Rabbi Joshua Saltzman, told me that when a very learned and venerable rabbi was asked about the problems with xtianity, he said, "Christians are confused" and so they are and no wonder. This process might have greatly accelerated with Heathenism further ahead if it wasn't for the Nazi perversion of our traditions, think about it........ Finally now, Germanic Heathens have a birth right to their tribal traditions. This is an undeniable right, and we see now the destructive results of its denial to us and our Volk.

Valulfr: Finally, how much latitude in design should the aspiring Hexologist
employ in the construction of the Hex-sign?

Hunter: I have vowed to not only to preserve the tradition of painting hexafoos, but to extend it into the future as a viable international art form. I have compared it to the Delta Blues, as a form it is very simple, anybody can do it. Hexology accomodates any system of symbology, however the northern tradition of Galdr staves from Iceland , a far more sophisticated system by the way suits it very well, so I have decided to leave the ancient Imperialistic Mediterranean Cultures symbology at the door in favor of a more Germanic tribal pantheon as well as one generated by the 'Blantz' and the Gods know what else, LOL....Heck the Wiccans have
 used them, The Celts have, Lee Gandee used the Kabalistic, arcane symbology! Hexology accommodates it all. These things are cosmograms, short form cosmologies. In all cultures, the division of a circle into six and eight parts and their variants are used to describe the 'Living Universe' A folk artist, I am not. A Cosmologist? in Deitsch we call them Hexologists.

Waldzauberer Interview with Hunter Yoder

Today I thank Waldzauberer for coming on and conversing with me, from one Hex to another. He's had quite a year, also known as Valúlfr, Óðvaknir, Jaivanta, and many other by-names, his experience in the realms of Hexerei and Icelandic Galdr are legendary. We had the pleasure of showing Hexes together this year at Germ Bookstore/Gallery in Philadelphia in a show entitled, "Deitsch Heathen Hexology" Anyway first Question:

1.Heil Waldzauberer! Tell what you can about the reasons behind the disbanding of your well known Rune School, The Wolfbund?

* The reasons were legion my friend, suffice to say that between losing friends over disjointed and out of control egos to getting folks who really didn't know what it was to be a "magician", the Wolfbund had seen its days, at least I'd had enough of it all. There were also health issues that had manifested that needed my undivided attention, so everything unfolded as it should have. Through it all my personal Work continues on nonetheless, such is the life of a Hex, I'm just a lot more cautious now about who I choose to pass along what I have learned over the past 34 years.

2. You seem to have been able to compartmentalize the

Hexerei from the Galdrstaves in your work, is that correct and if so what can you say about that?

* For me, this is an ongoing process of discovery and innovation. Starting off with the painting of Hexefuus, I decided to stick with "original" motifs to get a real feel for the craft itself. Given all the potential in shape, form, and color, I think this was the best approach for how I'm wired. My background in Icelandic galdrstaves as you know is extensive. Normally these are scratched on wood and stained with some special substance, or they are penned on specific medium. To date, I have successfully married the two "systems" in my mind, with some very positive feedback on my most recent piece, the Vegvisir–hex. Your work in this area obviously served as the inspiration for my own

3. We have discussed at length the PA Deitsch traditions. I can't but notice the enormous Germanic energies emanating from Michigan, educate us.

* Aside from my own endeavors here in the Great Lakes region over the years, and the already established heathen communities, there are those who had their genesis in my hallowed Hall going all the way back to the mid 90's that continue the Work today. Some of them have now established themselves in independent Halls that are somewhat philosophically connected, others are either solitary or have joined other groups; all are completely independent of what was the Wolfbund.

It's like a tree you grow and nurture; it will produce seeds that fall whereby new trees will grow, and though they look somewhat similar to the old tree, they are unique unto themselves nonetheless; this is a feature of Berkano. All in all, I don't think this is unique to the Great Lakes area though, there seems to be a strong surge of heathenism across the country, amazing what the internet has done.

4. The folkish Germanic Heathen community has embraced Hexology, any thoughts?

* Symbols are a very interesting study in how they impact the consciousness of man. The hex-sign seems to resonate on a very deep level with those of German descent for obvious reasons. Additionally, due to its obscurity, it has a certain draw and mystique that connects many to a piece of German-American history that can still be seen in your neck of the woods. It's also something that Deutsch/Deitsch folk can embrace today, keeping the craft itself alive and well. Hopefully we won't see them in video games like runes are today.

5. As a fellow enthusiast of wood and iron fittings from old structures, what is it about these materials?

* Good question, I'm really not sure though. I have been drawn to old structures since I was a kid growing up in rural Michigan. I would come across some old barn, or house, and find a quiet place to sit, listen and "feel". For me, it was as if I could almost hear the past whispering through what was left; a resonance, or signature that imprints itself on its surroundings. A

great many "workings" have taken place amid such places. I suppose it's also an appreciation of the craftsmanship of days gone by. My Grandfather was a carpenter, old school, and I remember when he got out of the business, and how pissed off he was at the new way of building homes and barns.

6. What is the relationship between Germanic Folkish Heathenry, the religion, and Hexerei?

* Difficult question for me to answer as I am not involved in any organized Folkish groups, however, on the surface it's really a question about the relationship between religion and magic. To me, religion, regardless of the flavor, is a belief system based upon a concept that a divine cosmic being can/will act on one's behalf under the right set of circumstances of a devotional nature. Magic, on the other hand, and generally speaking, is the belief that the developed human Will can bring about changes, both internally and externally, in accordance with desire and need. One is not any better than another; it's really a matter of one's temperament and world-view. For the religionist, symbols serve to remind one of ones place in the grand scheme of things, and for the magician (Hex), symbols serve their creator to effect change in the world(s) around and in them.

7. The Rune School concept of the subjective/objective Universe in Galdrstaves and Hexology, is it that simplistic. Isn't this Dualism? My view is that the concept is overplayed, what is yours?

* Unfortunately, dualism is the springboard from which we all start our lives. It is the prevailing philosophy that is difficult to overcome except for the few. Given this circumstance, and the fact that even our various languages have this undercurrent in it, it is the

philosophy of dualism itself that is used to peer beyond it. One must understand one's circumstance first before progress can be made. Over time, and with a good deal of re-wiring, the difference between what is called objective and subjective begins to blur. The galdor-stave, runes, hexefoos, what have you, are now seen as active "agents" working on behalf of the magician as co-creator/destroyer manifesting a directed Will.

8. At what point do the Northern European traditions part from our own New World/Vinlandish folk traditions and which way should we go with that?

*The first place I would start would be a healthy dose of reality. First and foremost none of us can be purists in the strictest sense of the term; we do not live in the 9th century. Granted, there is a good deal we can do within the cultural norms we live in today, but there is a good deal we cannot as well. Our social niceties have changed radically in the past 120 years; hel, there was a time when hangings were public affairs where the whole community would attend. I wonder how many folk today could endure watching this for an afternoon. Anyway, regarding the issue of Northern European vs. Vinlandish tradition, I don't see this as a problem in that the Vinlandic traditions were actually brought here by our ancestors from whatever part of Europe they came from. Additionally, there was a good deal of borrowing from the native populations which is evidenced in many of the early American farming, hunting, and healing folk traditions. This too, I believe is making a quiet comeback. As far as which way to go; I say, go with your blood, what will work will resonate with you, and be sure to teach the young ones.

9. What influences, if any did Kabbalah have on Icelandic Magic?

* That, of course, depends on what period in their history we look at. Prior to the conversion of 1000 CE there was virtually no influence as the population was composed largely of heathen Norwegians and Celts from Ireland, its only after the conversion that things get interesting with regard to your question. With the coming of the first Catholic Bishops to Iceland came knowledge of all sorts from the continent, travel to and from the continent also increased, mostly by those who could afford it. At any rate, knowledge was passing back and forth among the educated; this includes those interested in the arcane. Several of the most well known "Magicians" from that period were Bishops, and with them came the occidental traditions, such as they were at the time. There are examples of SATOR squares from Iceland, some carved in runic script, there are also elements of Judeo/Christian motifs in many of the magical formula, as well as the "Himmelsbrief", or Letter to/or from Heaven. This is not unusual to Iceland though, that pattern is repeated all over Europe during the transition period relative to the area.

10. I've drawn blanks in the Germanic/Rune School arena for my personal interest in Shamanism. What tribal primitive Germanic practices fill that void?

* There are many in fact, that's if we are defining

"shamanism" the same way. When I think of Shamanism, I think of the tribal traditions of the pan-Eurasian semi-polar people, I think of the pan-American "medicine-man", the Bon of Tibet, and so on. One common thread with the "traditional" tribal Shaman, regardless of place of origin is; communication with the dead, healing an afflicted person through "spirit travel" and/or plant knowledge, foretelling the future, the perspective that all of nature is animate, shape-shifting into various animals, song/chant/galdr/mantra/etc, direct communication via a meta-language with the "spirits" and animals of the tribe and geographic area, and last, but not the end of a longer list, a unique world-view that places the Shaman at the direct "center" of his/her world. This view is the most important factor for the rest of it to work.

So in answer to your question, there are a variety of "shamanistic" type practices from our ancient Germanic past that can still be invoked today, the problem being in the label and the various understandings of the terms used. However, from the list above, one can see that there are practices from our Germanic past via the literature that have similar descriptions. For example, if I use the Old Icelandic term *seið-berendr*, meaning sorcery, or one who communicates with the dead, well what does that mean? Sorcery means different things to folks, and besides, that's a Latinized French term used to describe some practice from Iceland that was similar to what was called sorcery on the continent. Even the "shamans" of Finland and of the Siberian tribes were called "sorcerers" by the Christian missionaries. All in all, I think that our collective Germanic heathen "spirit" has awakened, and a good deal of the "old ways" have begun to reemerge. It will look different though, as it should; we don't live in that time any longer.

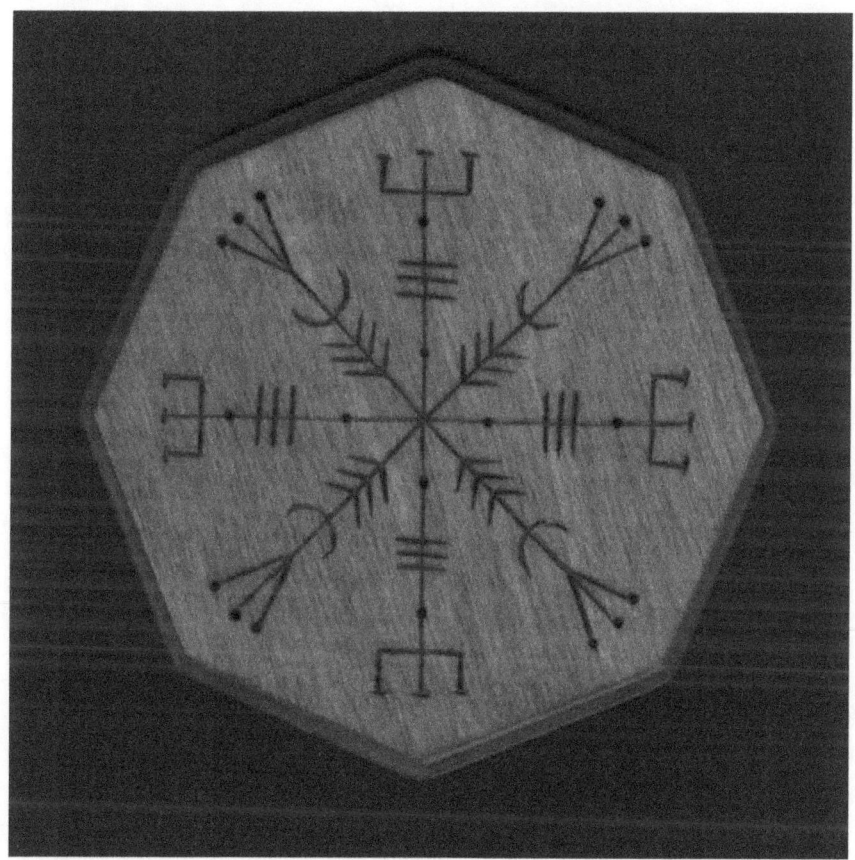

11. How do the magic objects you create differ from their images that we see on the internet?

* To me, and this is just my humble opinion, having "the object" within your personal sphere creates a resonance

between the two. This includes something for one's self, or something meant for another, this is the basic rule of sympathetic magic. There are of course other possibilities that could include optical magic, something I became aware of recently. Seems a mutual online friend of ours from Texas had some very positive reactions from simply looking at the Vegvisir-hex online.

12. The older more primal symbols used in Hexology such as the rosette, the cross, the spiral, the earthstar, etc. what is their relationship to Runology?

* Not much from what I can tell, with the exception of the use of symbols to represent specific ideas. However, that has now changed, today, with Hexologists such as yourself, a "marriage" between the two has emerged. We, who are using the best of both worlds in our rendering of Hexefuus, are on the cutting edge of what will come of it.

13. Plant mysticism in Germanic Heathen traditions today seems to have been forgotten. What are your views on 'die Blantz' ?

* Oh, I don't know, I think there are a lot more Folks paying attention to die Blantz, at least the well grounded "heathen". To me, and you know this, plants are sacred things, been a big fan of die Blantz for over 30 years, especially those with a "strong spirit". There are plants that can take you places only imagined, plants that heal or kill. After having grown Datura now for a couple of years, I can now say that we have gotten to know each

other quit well. Among the "power" plants I'm growing are Henbane (*Hyoscyamus niger*), *Atropa* belladonna, and tobacco (*Nicotiana*), all Solanaceae family. I have also made it a point to learn what grows within a quarter mile of where I live, something every Vinlandic heathen should do.

Interview with Hexenfrau Swanhilde with Hunter Yoder

'Weather Hex', Swanhilde, 2009

Heil der Swan
As promised the questions......
I have the pleasure of interviewing Hexenfrau Swanhilde, one of the leading Deitsch Heathen Hexologists today, who along with her husband, Valulfr Vaerulsson, combine to create the hexafoos in the traditional manner with something extra, Anyway Swan, first question.

Your work has an intensity to it which is remininscent to me of the Northern Rennaissance minatures of the Flemish masters who worked in egg tempura and egg oil tempura, How do you get that intensity into your work?

I am unsure if you are referring to the color usage or the small detail so I will answer from the perspective of both concepts. As for colors, the Renaissance period in art had an intense richness and depth to the colors. They were also masters at the use of the principle of simultaneous contrast to enhance the depth and shades of colors. This technique is based on the way that the eye perceives colors when placed next to another color. For example you can take one color and when it is placed next to several colors your eye will perceive it differently next to each color. This is one of the primary design aspects that I utilize when painting. Having worked for Sherwin Williams for ten years, I have a firm grasp on colors and what is necessary to make a color and what colors work to enhance other colors.

Everything boils down to color for me. Even when I make a salad, I base the ingredients on color not flavor. As I have evolved as a hexologist, I have noticed that this intensity of color that you speak of has grown by leaps and bounds.

As for the detail work, I have always worked small. My art professor used to get on me about that all of the time. "You need to work bigger" he would say. I have worked both ends of that spectrum, but I do like the minute details. I have been doing that since childhood, filling up notebook paper with tiny little drawings. One childhood activity that left a major impression on me was the art of Ukrainian Eggs at Easter after my brother and I outgrew the Easter Bunny. In the making of the hexes, I utilize the sense of design that I have built upon as an adult through art training and working with interior design. While I can attribute it to this or that, most of what you see from me is essentially an innate ability.

Many of your traditional designs are based on Hexenmeister Lee R. Gandee's own. What attracts you to his work?

This is difficult to answer in a short response. I have been drawn strongly to his work even before I knew it was his, or even who he was. I have been drawn on and off over the years to this art, but I will always consider his work to be my favorite. As my understanding of this craft has increased, and I have now read his book "Strange Experience" (and I thank you for that), I find that my draw to his designs is even stronger. I have been working with the craft of rune magic for eighteen years and have attained a level of mastery. When I look at his hexes, I can see the rich blend of the art and the magic, and I somehow understand them. I see many that have lost touch with the magic and I see them as simply a folk art. His work incites sensation within me on a very deep level. They are very powerful even though they are in black and white. Now that I know more about the man, I see similarities between him and I. As I grew up, there were certain aspects of my personality that I had kept to myself. In urban areas, there was little tolerance for the "old ways". Being that most of the populace had no sense of these things, I was seen as "odd". Fortunately my mother was "odd" too but hers was squelched by her mother with a switch. In many ways she fostered in me that which she could not express without being beaten as a child. When I was about three I took a purple crayon and drew on the wall in the upstairs hall. She never cleaned it off because, as she puts it, she was amazed because it reminded her of primitive art. While she never allowed herself to explore her magical leanings beyond the intellectualization of various systems, she never stood in my way and fostered me in looking beyond the social norm. But I digress. I would have liked to meet Mr. Gandee, to learn from him. The main thing that I did learn from his book is that I need to trust my instincts.

Can you share with us to some degree how you activate

your hexafoos?

They actually are activated even before any paint is spread. In my experience they have a life of their own, and the energy that they contain exists before they are visually represented, and I am the conduit to the expression of that energy. I approach each one in a ritual manner. I always have a candle lit, and I have recently begun to wear a straw hat while painting. It is my gardening hat, which makes it an article of clothing associated with gestation and growth. When working on one for an individual, I ask them for three key words to express their desired effect. I actually can express energies and emotions visually much better than I can with words. I recently completed a personal hex which is geared towards the magical process and creative spark that led me to and has assisted me in this form of magic and art. This piece was activated in a different manner than the others because of its personal nature. It was tied to me and I to it in a ritualistic manner, the details of which will remain unsaid. It will appear in the show at Germ in February 2009, but will not be for sale. To date, I see it as my most powerful piece to date.

I know that there is a 'count' in your work, especially in the borders, what role does the numerology play in your work?

Ah yes, that there is. I am very much aware of the

numerology as it applies to the runes, and I will integrate runic elements through the numbers within the patterns. Many times I will use the number twenty-four in the borders denoting the number of runes in the elder futhark. Also by using twenty-four each point or scallop falls every fifteen degrees and fifteen denotes the rune elhaz which represents protection. Fifteen times 24 equals 360, which will break down in this manner 3+6+0 = 9 = hagalaz or transformation. There are also universal numerical principles which I will get into more in the next question. Suffice it to say that I have always had a head for math and the patterns that exist numerically.

What are your feelings about six as compared to eight pointed stars? Do you prefer one over the other?

First I would like to address some numerical principles. What I have in mind are the symbolic representations of the numbers three and four. The number four, in many traditions, represents those things which are bound by the laws of nature or the physical. Three represents spiritual matters which are far more malleable and intangible in nature. Both of the stars that you asked about are twofold aspects of these paradigms, and can be viewed through this lens.
I like them both and use them in pieces where the desired effect warrants them. One of my favorites though, is the twelve which we have discussed before. It

has a combination of both three and four. I really cannot say that I like one over another, because I love them all. It is all pieces of a larger picture that most never conceive of beyond their own piece of the puzzle. By utilizing all of these principals we begin to see dimensionally rather than flat like a puzzle on a card table.

Your work uses symbology sparingly yet the intention is clear, how do you do that?
Does the color combinations you use substitute for symbolism?

I guess that I had not thought about it, but you are right. I tend to work more with the geometrical designs rather than symbology. There is something that has occurred to me since working in this medium that you may find interesting. I have been performing rune readings for about seventeen years. My talent is that I am empathic. The readings generally are extremely personal in nature as a result. More times than not, when I am performing a reading for an individual, I receive the "messages" in a geometric form, and I have to decipher what emotions it evokes in me. Before I began working with and learning hexology I did not understand why this happened, and I have never met any other reader who has a similar occurrence. I still do not know how or why this happens, but I believe that it directly ties into my ability to create powerful hexes without the use of symbology. I do use various symbols from time to time, but I am more strongly drawn to the geometrics. The colors play a major role in conveying the purpose to the viewer on a subliminal level allowing them to "feel" the meaning. An interesting side note to this is that while discussing this question and answer with Valulfr, he put out a theory. He postulated that when I receive these geometrical patterns that I am seeing their fetch, and that where most people see them as animals, that I see them as geometrical patterns. I believe that he is right. It is amazing how we can know so much and always have room to learn and achieve higher levels of perception and understanding.

What comparisons can be made between the Deitsch Hexafoos tradition and the Icelandic Galdrastafir tradition? How closely related are they?

There are similarities and differences in both traditions. While they essentially evolved in separate regions, they both stem from an Indo-European psychology. They both utilize a similar field principle in that there is a rule of three in the breakdown of the circle that contains the glyphs. Working from the center point outwards there is the inner self, then the second or the realm that merges the outside influences with the inner, finally the outside influences, or the outer edge of the circle. Where the Galdrastafir were a more secret art, utilized by magicians, the hexafoos were employed by the folk , their display being more prominent. They are both magical arts yet the hexafoos is more acceptable due to the perception by outsiders that they are purely decorative in nature. This allowed the German folk to be surrounded by magical art without fear. Over time, they have seemed to devolve into a more decorative art except in small pockets of the population. I do see them as related yet they evolved differently based on localized cultural influences.

Can you explain Gandee's "Eye of God" design? Is it his original design or is it based on an older one? I don't 'feel' that one, what am I missing?

As a child I used to make these things out of sticks and yarn. I have looked into their origin, and what I can figure out regarding this question and the Gandee design, is that he picked this design up during his time in Mexico, as the craft is found there and in Bolivia. It could be that you do not feel a connection to it because it is not a design of Germanic origin. I have made two of this design thus far. While I initially had the same opinion of this design as you have expressed, when I made it for Jack Montgomery, I found the experience quite powerful, and it left me with a massive headache that appeared each time I reproached it to put the last touches on it. Because of the nature of the piece's use, and the profound effect it had on me, I have opted not to post that particular one in my portfolio. I have no wish to lessen its power in any way.

As a Seidkhona, what connection is there between Seidhr and making Hexafoos?

This is an interesting question Hunter. I have pondered this question longer than any of the others. It touches on a mystery that I have wrestled with for many years. Let me lay out a basic idea of what I believe about seidhr based upon my years of contemplation. Seidhr is a form of active magic that is performed by achieving an ecstatic state, the means and method of which are sketchy at best. I find that many believe that foretelling or Spæ craft is seidhr. This is a form of passive magic and just does not fit with the lore. One point that I get stuck on that relates to this stance is that it is written that Freyja was the possessor of this art and that Odhinn learned it from her. It is also written that Odhinn possesses a chair that while sitting in it can foresee. Why would he need to gain this knowledge if he could already do this. There are many questions that have no answers regarding Seidhr and no one can claim the true use of this craft.
If I approach this question from the perspective of my views on this subject, which in reality I could go on about for a long while but will keep brief for these purposes, I would say that there are some similarities. I have found that when creating a hexafoos with an intended purpose and owner, I enter a state that is quasi-trancelike. While I am aware of my surroundings as they

are, if someone speaks to me, I will hear their voice but not the words, and in some cases I will not understand their words. The energy that flows through me into the hexefoos is very strong and the recognizable sensations that it triggers vary but are extremely intense (ecstatic). The designs and colors flow out onto the wood with great ease and speed and the piece takes on a vibration of its own and so far have seemed to worked their intent well. With a working of seidhr, I would require an outside stimulus to achieve such a state and effect. With the hexefoos, I become one with the wood and paint stimulating the energy in it as much as the piece creates it in me. As I transform the wood, it transforms me!

Lastly when using hearts in a hexafoos, should they point inward or outward?

That would depend entirely on the creator's intent with the energy they symbolize. That is whether they wish to draw it in or send it out. With all symbols, the placement and orientation can denote different aspects of their representation. So my answer is "yes".

Eric Claypoole, Berks County Hexologist Interview with Hunter Yoder

Today I have the privilege of interviewing the current reigning Meister of Hexology, Eric Claypoole,
"He is carrying on a long family tradition. Johnny Claypoole, his father, began painting hexsigns in 1962. Johnny was taught by the legendary Johnny Ott, the self-proclaimed "Dr. of Hexology". Johnny's career in painting hexsigns spanned nearly four decades. He was featured on the Charles Kuralt "On the Road" program and on the game show :What's my Line?". He was also a regular on the Captain Noah children's program. Johnny and Eric have been exhibiting their wares at the Kutztown Folk Festival continually since 1962."

"Shortly before his father's death in 2004, Eric took over the family business, including painting the traditional designs on barns. He lectures on the history of barnstars and hexsigns as well. Eric is one of the few remaining barnstar painters in the country"

Eric has been featured in the New York Times http://www.nytimes.com/2006/07/22/us/22hex.html?_r=1&n=Top/Reference/Times%20Topics/Subjects/B/Barns

I had the pleasure of being a friend of the Claypoole family as a young man and went to high school with Mark and Kevin. Eric was quite abit younger and the family was large, all boys if I recall correctly with one long suffering sister, Faith. Anyway this was the late sixties and early seventies. So here we go.

1. Hey Eric, Recently when in Philadelphia, I ran into some of Johnny's Hexes at the Terminal Market in Center City. Tell us something about Johnny's connection to 'The City of Brotherly Love'

johnny grew up in upper darby and moved to berks county after ww2 he bought the farm and moved up a few years later. after he took over johnny ott's business,,he did shows in philly at gimbels and philly folk festival and reading terminal market where he met mike who owns the general store. mike has sold his signs there for a number of years.

2. What stories can you recount about Johnny and Johnny's relationship? (Johnny Claypoole/ Johnny Ott)

my dad was a welder for many years always trying to find himself going from job to job looking for his nitch. he was always fasinated with the barnstars and one day came across an add in the paper from johnny ott looking for an apprentice. johnny ott took to him and showed him how to paint in 1962. when he died 2 years later,,my dad took over his legacy and started at the kutztown folk festival in 1965.

3. The first set of 'Barn Charms' I repainted were on my Dad's barn about a mile or two from Virginville, I believe they were Milton Hill's They were embossed right into the barnsiding, Eight pointers with a outer

border of curly que lines and raindrops between the rays. What can you tell us about Milton and his work? Did he invent that spiral Hex sign?

Milton Hill, collection of Eric Claypoole

miltonhill was a barn painter and too my knowledge was comissioned by the hex tour in the 40's to repaint the barnstars around the hex highway area and surrounding towns. my calculations tell me he was born in 1888,,i met 2 of his daughters,,they were touching 90 when i talked to them.ester derr still lives in virginville and i talked with her after working on her house. she told me alot about her father and thanked me for my father naming one of his signs "the hill star" as a young boy he was fascinated with star designs and was incuraged to draw them in school around the turn of the century. i held one he drew when he was about 12. she gave me some pictures of him to photo copy and told me alot about him. in my opinion,,milton hill was the most phonimenal barnstar painter there will ever be,,his designs were very detailed.milton only painted stars and rosettes and coined the phrase "chust fer nice" milton hill was comissioned by the first folk festival to demonstrate barnstar painting. tourists wanted to take them home so they started painting them on disks for the following year,,some say johnny ott was the first to paint on a disk. the name "hex sign" was coined by wallace nutting in 1923 in his book,,"pennsylvania beautiful" but the first hex sign sold on a disk was pretty much believed to be sold at the 2nd folk festival by milton hill. johnny ott started what i call the modern hexsign with hearts,birds and tulips on them. all those symbols came from the fraktur art,,marriage and birth certificates and decorated tolewareand dowry chests. the symbols used represented positive things out of the bible,,hearts meant love,tulips represented faith ,hope and charity,,bluebirds of peace and happiness,,distlefinks(thistlefinch,gold finch) for prosperity. borders represented smooth sailing through life. the star design is as old as time,,the dutch didn't invent it and they didn't give hex signs to each other as gifts. the hexsign was created at the folk festival,,the barnstar painted on barns is over 200 years old.there were no names of hex sign or barnstar back then,,only stunna (stars) and blumma(flowers) for the barns. it is my belief that they started out as date boards built in the stone gable ends of barns usually with a star design , initials and the date the barn was built. the oldest barnstar i repainted is 1819 just 1 mile north of lenhartsville. historian and folk art specialist don yoder believes the were painted around the end of the civil war,,but that is when alot of barns were painted red,,paint was mass produced and cheaper.priar to that,,barns weren't painted,,but the star design eventually were painted on the forebays in the 1830' and 40's. the "ghost" of a barnstar and the gable end recesses of barnstars and "dateboards" are the proof in my opinion that they are 50-60 years older then yoder believes. we have showed him pictures and gable end recesses and he is now curious about them.there are no pictures of them in his book but we have found about 40 barns with evidence of gable end recess barnstars since i repainted the one in lenhartsville. patrick dunmoyer has found one just out of bally in montgomery county that we believe in 1786. we have toured alot together looking at barns along with bob emsminger and greg huber,,barn specialists.

Eric's testing site for Hex sign 'weathering'

4. How important are your outer borders on the circumference of you Hex signs? What different styles are there and are they just a showcase for the artist's abilities and inventiveness?

borders we to represent smooth sailing through life. alot were solid black borders but we found alot of scalloped and saw tooth(mostly in lehigh county) slash marks in a triangular pattern were common around here. i was told 10 years ago that my hex signs had to have 22 scallops around the border,,the were called water wheels. i have since painted mostly every sign with 22 scallope around it,,11 on either side of the half circle.

5. In between the rays of your barnstars I believe you

use equilateral crosses frequently, do they function just as a place holder or is there a symbolic purpose?

the 12 point star has always been my favorite barnstar,, now i call it the perfect geometrical form. when layed out properly,,it has every common angle known to man. i believe the 30'60'90 square came from this design and was told it was the basis for every foundation used to build the cathederals in europe. you can connect points to have a perfect equilateral rectangle,,triangle and square. the 12 points represented the 12 apostles,,the pinwheel in the center was people spinning through time and the rosetters (the crosses you mentioned) 4 point stars if you will were to ward off evil disease and pestilants. the red dot was to represent christs blood.

6. Has there been a change in attitudes amongst the 'PA Dutch' regarding the magical aspects of Hexology? The old school crew would always dismiss Barnstars as being "chust for nice"

i believe meanings and representations could easily have changed over the years from generation to generation just from saying,,i think granpa said this meant this and one or 2 words different could change things. i think they were symbolic to them,,basic good luck good health and prosperity,,fertility and protection from lightning. there is alot of whitch stories attributed to them,,legond or wivestales,,i don't know the truth but i think the "witch doors"(doors painted on the barns) on barns were simply to make it look symetrical. i do hear alot of witch stories at the folk festival.

7. I recall as a young man in Berks County feeling a connection between Hex Signs and the Blue Mountains. It seemed that the closer to the Mts I got, the more elaborate and intense the Hexes would become. I know you live closeby to those Mts, The Deitsch Eck and such, whats your take on that?

the dutch immergrated from germantown north to the blue mountains leaving their barns in every county north of philly to here. at one time berks county went from philly to new your border. the indians were pushed over the mountain but berks county as we know it reminded them of their homeland. some say the distlefink looking backwards was symbolic of them looking back at the homeland. i have seen alot of elaborate barns all over and in the south mountain area. lehigh and berks have so many but berks seems to be the epicenter of barnstars.

8. Do you recall or have you heard of "Bumbaugh" or Mt Bummy?
i remember him from the folk festival as i was very young then,,but my dad knew him pretty well,,he was quite a charactor and he was quite the ladies man as i have been told. he was said to be an erbalist and possibly skilled in the pow wow mysteries.

9. I recall your whole family painting signs in preparation for various festivals including the Philly Folk Festival, The Kutztown Folk Festival back in the late sixties early seventies and Johnny packing em all up in his VW Microbus Any thoughts regarding Hexology and Psychedelia or those times?
just a coincedence with psychedilia and the 70's

10. I saw thos pics on your site of your work on stone animals. Whats going on there? Is it the animals or the stones that seems to have a certain power?

i repainted the distlefink at the heritage center in reading a few years ago,,it is cast aluminum and was donated in 1984. my father painted a daddy hex on the eyes and a few other artists painted the rest. ruthan hartung did the designs and i repainted it close to what she wanted but much brighter anc colorful. the bear on my website is one of the boyertown bears (www.bearfever.org) it is a fiberglass form from chicago made by cowpainters. the first ones there were cows in chicago said to represent the cow that kicked over the milk pail that knocked over the keroscene lamp that started the chicago fire.

11. Who has and where are the best collections of Hex Signs to your knowledge? Besides the Deitsch Eck Hotel, dining room, which I love, where are the Johnny Ott's today?
What do you consider your Father's best works?

the deitch eck is definately one of my favorites but milton hill will always be the most phoniminal star painted that ever lived,,i wish i had one of his. i held a few of them already.i have restored a number of barns painted by hill,,every star on the barn looks the same but each is individually different in a suttle way only milton hill could do. i have a collection of my fathers and a few otts in my studio. one of his friends has over 75 pieces of my dads. the folk festival has a nice collection of 4'ers. it is hard to say what is the best work of my fathers,,maybe his legacy keeping johnny otts work alive and passing on to me. the name claypoole is english,but his mother was pa dutch,,(steigerwalt) so he was half dutch. i consider myself 1/4 dutch as my mother was pure irish. i am only an artist,,but i am blessed with keeping up the tradition of hex signs and barnstars. i do lectures 10-12 times a year and have done 3 or 4 with patrick dunmoyer,,we became good friends over the last year. he is a very talented young man,,very well spoken,,very knowlegable on the history.

12. Any thoughts on Hexology internationally? How about the state of the Deitsch Kultur reawakening in Berks County?

hexology,,barnstars and hexsigns are what i consider to be a very interesting,,mystical,,sometimes contraversial ,extradornidary art form. the star is as old as time yet every culture has its beliefs in the powers of the star, whether it be mind over matter or the star with the astrological aspects and energy of the universe,,we will argue this forever. ask 10 old dutchmen about barnstars,,you will get 10 different answers. its all part of the art. life is a wonderful gift,,enjoy it everyday!! thanks,,,eric claypoole www.claypoolehexsigns.com

Eric Claypoole and Hunter Yoder, 2012

another minor point ,, hexsigns and barnstars have nothing to do with the amish,,although they came from the same areas of the platnate and switzerland and speak the same dutch dialect,,they are known as the plain people and paint their barns white. people ask me all the time,,are these amish? look on ebay,,you'll see why,,every silk screen says...amish dutch hex sign. the silk screen industry put meanings to everything and i learned the meanings growing up,,but i got to a point and said,,who says so,,so i started asking. i like to say what they represent,,not what they mean,,there is a big difference between hand painted and silk screens.
Many thanks Eric Claypoole!

Patrick Donmoyer, Berks County Hexologist and Scholar

With Hunter Yoder

Today in continuation of our "Interview Series" We have a fellow Berks County Hexologist and scholar on the subject, PATRICK DONMOYER. Patrick has recently graduated from my old Alma Mater, Kutztown University with a BFA in Fine Arts, as I have myself. And he has a minor in the new PA German Studies Program. He has distinguished himself with his Kutztown University Honors Thesis & Historic Hex Sign Survey of historic hex signs throughout Berks county and has an impressive resume of giving lectures on the subject. He has a wonderful site, http://www.paedrigdesign.com/ and without further ado, here we go.

1. Patrick, Give us some information on your extensive survey of Berks County Barnstars. Is the resource going to be available online or what plans do you have for publishing the results?

In the Summer of 2008, I began the process of driving all agricultural and rural roads in Berks County to document and photograph all visible examples of decorated barns. I did this with the generous support of the Peter Wentz Farmstead Society, who funded my project with a research scholarship. I mapped the locations of every site I documented, and photographed the barns, their decorations and any other features that seemed relevant to the search, including graffiti, interior decorations, and architectural features. In only about 20% of the documented sites was I allowed or invited to explore the interior of the barn. Despite this difficulty, I was surprised to be able to collect an immense amount of data from the interiors of barns taken from within only a small sample of my total survey results. In total, I collected photos of over 400 barns. I was pleasantly surprised by the number and diversity of the designs. My work has also to a lesser degree extended into Lehigh, Northampton, Bucks, Montgomery, Lebanon, Lancaster, Schuylkill and York Counties. I've taken thousands of photographs since I began. I've been offering lectures to historical, civic and educational organizations which are comprised of 45 minute photographic presentations outlining the results of my survey through the context of Pennsylvania Dutch Folklore.

I've also teamed up for continued field work and presentations with Eric Claypoole of Lenhartsville, the most prolific Barn Star Painter in Pennsylvania. Eric is single-handedly responsible for the vast majority of Berks County's historical repaintings as well as countless original works in Berks, Lehigh, & Montgomery Counties. Eric and I work to continue the process of documenting not only the historic evidence of the tradition, but I also make a point to document his activities as an artist because his work is exceptionally important for future generations. Very few historic photographs exist today showing a barn star painter of the past at work.

A sample of my research and artwork is available on my website www.paedrigdesign.com, and some are available through Kutztown University's Library at the Keystone Library Network's digital database located at http://klndigital.passhe.edu/. More of my work will be available in the future at the Research Library of the Pennsylvania German Cultural Heritage Center at Kutztown University.

After the first of the year, I will in earnest resume the writing of my collected work. I'm preparing a documentary volume that highlights photography of hundreds of locations along with a new assessment of the implications of the artistic tradition. It seems to me that only half of the story of their existence, use and meanings has been available to the public in a collected format. I'm interested in presenting a diversity of potential interpretations rooted in folklore rather than exclusively supporting one perspective. If there is one thing that I know for certain about the Pennsylvania Dutch, it is that there are always ideas and beliefs that remain unspoken, and no two people will offer exactly the same story.

2. What is your preference, Barnstars or Hex Signs and what are the differences?

For my purposes as a researcher, both of these terms are problematic from the very beginning. They are strictly anachronisms which bear little resemblance to the terminology used by those who came before us. Nevertheless, I prefer the words "Barn Stars" because the terminology is somewhat comparatively clear: I study illustrations of abstract celestial images painted on barns. I generally use the term Barn Star for the work actually painted on a barn. I make a distinction between this and commercial disks. I like the idea of referring to the images as "stars" because we know of only a few terms used in the Pennsylvania German Dialect for the designs, such as "die Blumme," "die Schtanne," and "die Blummeschtanne," meaning respectively, "flowers," "stars," and "flower-stars." Both of these terms reference the geometric content of earthly and celestial observations. Words such as "die Hexezeeche" and "die Scheier Schilder," when applied to barn decorations are all twentieth-century adaptations of English phrases. The terms cannot be found in any primary sources over one-hundred years old, and they have no historical connection to the tradition of painting stars on barns. "Die Hexezeeche" is a Pennsylvania Dutch adaptation of a earlier European German phrase which refers more directly to small-scale images created either for the purpose of protecting an individual or building from witchcraft, or smale-scale images created for the purpose of witchcraft. This type of activity can be seen in some markings found inside barns, homes and outbuildings, but it cannot be applied in a comprehensive sense to the large-scale designs on barns. To apply the term in this way would imply that the designs served a single standardized purpose, rather being a living tradition which communicates to the viewer on many levels. The designs on barns both historically and today have a diversity of meanings, and the idea of witchcraft-protection seems to be a comparatively recent interpretation of the designs. Ideas like blessing, fertility, and spiritual protection seem far older, and these implications can be traced to similar traditions in European vernacular architecture. The first documented case of the word "Hex" being used in conjunction with the designs is highly controversial. Wallace Nutting, a New Englander, coined the term "Hexefuss" in 1924, claiming to have heard it from a single source in Lehigh County. Nutting did not understand any Pennsylvania Dutch dialect in the slightest bit, and his story is therefore questionable. A common word used for the design of the six-pointed rosette in Germany is "die Sechstern." Another way of saying six-sided star in Pennsylvania is "sex-foosich Schtann." Could "sex-foosich" and "hexefoos" sound similar to an untrained ear? It is certainly possible. It is also possible that the farmer with whom Nutting was speaking was referring to something entirely different from the designs. I have heard the word Hexefuss used by older members of the PA Dutch community to describe a symbol of runic origin used for protection, also called a Gensefoos or Gruttefoos, as well as a popular tradition of making triangular cut-outs on door lintels which was believed to counter the entry of dangerous intruders. Never have I heard the word Hexefuss used by a native Pennsylvania Dutch dialect speaker to refer to the designs on barns. Another primary reason that I struggle to accept the word "Hex" in relation to the designs is that it carries a serious negative connotation in the Pennsylvania Dutch community. I do not believe that these designs would have been named after a negative force if they were used for protection. The words I have heard used to describe the stars taken from verbal accounts of Brauchers and Powwow practitioners are words like "Scheier Brauch," "painted prayers," "visual prayers." These are all terms aimed at a beneficial purpose. The only references to the word Hex in these discussions with powwow practitioners always carries a negative connotation, namely referring to a practitioner of Hexerei responsible for some ill-intention. Today, many people today use the word "hex" to mean any magical or shamanic activity. I have no problem with this use of the word as long as it is in a contemporary context of mutual agreement. Historically, it was simply not used the same way, and so it makes it difficult to communicate about the subject except in an anachronistic, anecdotal sense. If I went to an elderly powwow practitioner in Berks County and told him or her that I was interested in Hexerei, I would probably be turned away because the word carries a negative connotation. I try to seriously distinguish the difference between traditional paintings and hexerei in my own language.

3. Are they "Chust for nice"?

For some people, this is the only level that the designs can appreciated, and it is a persistent belief today. The only issue I have with the phrase is the "just" part, implying "only," which means they have no purpose other than their nicety. I have observed however, that there are a variety of beliefs present in the Pennsylvania Dutch community, some of which are simple, concrete, decorative interpretations, while others acknowledge beliefs, customs and rituals which are inter-related with the same symbolism. It appears to me that a generalized explanation simply cannot satisfy our culture's desire for clarification. My own approach to the subject is that I adhere only to a desire for clarification of ideas, based upon visual documentation and supportable terminology. I do not support one idea to the exclusion of all others. I have no problem acknowledging the fact that contradictory ideas exist within Pennsylvania Dutch culture. It is part of a culture's identity to have contradictions. These contradictions do not have to mean that someone is wrong and someone is right. It simply means that different people have different experiences with the same material.

4. And although Milton Hill is attributed with the above quote, what can you tell us about that great Virginville Hexologist?

Milton Hill is credited with being responsible for some of the most complex designs which can be found in Berks County, primarily in Winsor Castle, Edenburg, Virginville and the Hamburg area. His work normally features star patterns of alternating contrasting colors, receeding towards a central point, and bordered by complex overlapping arcs. His borders appear to form a lattice of diamond shapes which are often colored in a graduated scheme from darkest at the interior to lightest at the outermost edge. It is obvious to me however that Hill could not possibly be responsible for all of these designs which many people today call "Hill Stars." I know of a photograph of a barn in Windsor Castle from 1902, with the exact designs which later became Hill's signature arrangement. Hill was born in 1895, and he couldn't have produced these early examples. Hill is however responsible for making these designs flourish, and for re-combining the geometry in complex and innovative ways. Eric Claypoole of Lenhartsville has repainted and restored numerous designs believed to have been originally executed by Milton Hill because of the scribing technique used in the original layout. Milton Hill was a complex individual, and his contribution to the tradition in Berks County is unmistakable. I also find it exciting that his orientation is vastly different from my own, in that he saw the designs as purely decorative, yet his work stands out to me as some of the most captivating. I have an immense amount of respect for him as an artist.

5. Is Johnny Ott's work still visible today?

Only in the Deitsch Eck, and on masonite disks which can still be found hanging outside in some areas around Lenhartsville. I've only ever seen one or two of his disks on exterior architecture. They are too valuable to hang outside and weather away to nothing. Johnny Ott never actually painted a single barn. He painted disks that later were hung on barns, but very little evidence of his work exists outside of private collections. Ott's story is somewhat problematic historically. News articles from the 1950's refer to his work as being "Cabalistic Marks" - yet I study the Kaballah and some medieval diagramatical works illustrating sacred concepts and there is no relation between the Kaballah and Ott's work. Yet Ott claimed his work had a magical intention. Having studied the history of occult and ceremonial diagrams, I do not see much of any similarity at all between his work and the work of occultists. His work appears to be largely derived from his earlier artistic work which was decorated tinware - tolepainting. He is responsible for transforming the tradition of star painting by incorporating non-geometric elements, such as birds, and some of the less-geometrically oriented floral embellishments which normally appeared on tinware. And yet... he never claimed that his tinware had any magical content, nor has anyone suggested that his tinware was covered with "cabalistic marks." I'm not entirely sold on every aspect of his legendary persona. I might feel differently if I had met him in person, but I'll never know. I'm sure he must have been a very interesting person, to be sure. Usually, I am less attracted to his work than I am to other painters who focused more extensively on geometric pattern. His work is also less relevant to my study, as he never painted directly on any historic barns. Although, my favorite piece of Ott's is an abstract painting entitled "The Wild Lettuce Feeding It's

Young." This piece is the only work that I know of which appears to have an occult dimension. It was featured on an old postcard which is a part of my friend Eric Claypoole's private collection, but the original Ott painting seems to have vanished...

6. How do you feel about the much more recent practice of silk screened reproductions? I know that Ivan Hoyt licenses his work out in that way.

I don't have much of an opinion about it, because it accomplishes a completely commercial aim: the process is intended to mass-manufacture something to sell to tourists. Tourism is important to our local economy, so I respect it. But I also think that silk-screened designs are inferior fundamentally to hand-painted designs. I own an excellent Ivan Hoyt original that I keep in my car, but I never would have purchased it if it had been silk-screened.

I'm less critical of the silk-screened disks than I am of the literature that usually accompanies the disks in tourist shops. Much of the literature makes the false claim that the highly embellished floral and bird motifs are traditional designs painted on barns. This has never really been the case. Most of this work has more in common with painted tinware, while the oldest of the Barn Stars are all geometric. The Tourist literature also misleads the unknowing consumer into believing that the Pennsylvania Dutch created elaborate symbols which could be summed up in simple quaint phrases such as "good luck" and "love and romance." I know that today many people who collect these disk designs use these terms to differentiate the most popular of the post-1950 designs, and this surely makes sense in this context. For instance, the popular "Irish-hex," "the Daddy Hex," "Love and Romance" are titles used by Jacob Zook and Johnny Ott for very specific designs, and they were also some of the same titles used by Johnny Claypoole as Ott's student. These titles really only existed after 1950. I would not use the same terms to describe the historic designs. I tend to think that the explanations are far more complex.

7. It appears that you view Barnstars/Hexology as a form of cosmogram. What leads you to that interpretation?

I see cosmological implications as being the fulcrum of my research, and I attempt to understand it from two different perspectives. From the perspective of folklore, I've found loads of evidence to explain the use of astrological concepts in agricultural life, and I see this as the basis for explaining the significance of celestial activities to the Pennsylvania Dutch cultural context. I think this avenue has its limitations, however, as the designs rarely reference specific celestial bodies, but rather, they favor an astrological aesthetic, that is, the designs reference an interest in the celestial, and a reverence for the celestial. The designs are cyclically abstract, regular, and radially symmetrical. These attributes make them visually interesting and especially attractive to people whose beliefs favor the idea of an ordered universe. No matter what we believe today, we have to remember that the Pennsylvania Dutch in the past were mostly Protestants with a folk spirituality which was often interwoven with mystical beliefs. This set of beliefs can be used to inform our observations of the historic designs. I do not believe however that everyone who painted these designs on barns, or carved similar designs on tombstones, or decorated their furniture with geometric designs was conscious of this process.

8. Besides your expertise on Barnstars, you also are well informed on the subject of the architectural development of the PA German Bankbarn. What other marks have you found inside or out on these great structures?

I've found a number of different interior designs which closely resemble the exterior paintings. These range from the simplest of scribed rosettes to far more elaborate painted designs. Many of these are located by areas of transition, next to doors, or windows, or the entrances to granaries. I've also found a range of unexplained geometric designs which I am to this day uncertain of their implications. For these examples, to assume that I could re-assemble a meaning from my own set of modern-day attitudes would be misleading. I can't arbitrarily assign a meaning, even if I have a hunch of what something might mean. Many of them appear to be within the realm of Christian iconography, but there is a margin of doubt. I'm interested in ritual markings as well. I've photographed the historic use of crosses in groups of three, and sometimes the initials of Christ. I've also found crosses combined with other geometric and religious designs. Occasionally, I've found designs of a runic nature, however, I must warn that these designs are never found in context with other runes, only in isolation. This leads me to believe that the runes did not survive in a complete, cohesive system, but rather as ideograms which are isolated from the system as a whole, and therefore their meanings have changed somewhat. I've also found illustrations of animals, usually birds, occasionally livestock. I've seen illustrations of people, sometimes farmers, occasionally Indians. The most common things to find are tally-marks used for counting grain sacks, marriage marks (numbered hatch marks) to show how the various members of the timber frame are assembled, and initials of the barn owners and workers.

9. Any thoughts on the Northern European versions of Hex signs?

It would appear that nearly every culture of the world has some tradition of using geometric signs and symbols on their dwelling places, agricultural buildings, sacred sites and monuments. The designs used by the northern Europeans are no exception. I've never been to Europe - the information I've gathered comes from pictorial research from printed sources, as well as photographic examples given to me by fellow historians in the US and Germany. In general, I've found that European historians have less of a problem admitting possible

pagan associations with their decorative traditions. Especially prior to WWII, German historians had some interesting interpretations of their folk art. Many of these scholars emphasized the runic origins of some of the forms, as Germanic culture was experiencing a resurgence in interest in its mythology. Unfortunately the National Socialist movement usurped many of these designs for political emblems. It's no longer polite to talk seriously about the origins of some of these symbols. In many European countries it is illegal to use emblems such as the swastika, which were once very common in a folk context.
Nevertheless, the places that many of these early designs can be witnessed on folk architecture are in alpine regions of Switzerland, Germany, Austria. I've also seen similar designs in sources from Eastern Europe, the British Isles and Scandinavia.

10. Practitioners of Hexerei, or PA Germanic witchcraft energize a particulat object (Hex Sign) with a particular intent. This is done in various ways including the usage of bodily fluids especially blood. This view allows for only that particular object to carry the charge. Hexologists on the other hand would use red paint instead of blood and make the Hex so very good that its intent will travel throughout the 'universe' through any means including reproductions and the internet. What views do you have on this difference?

My experience with traditional geometric paintings has never led me to see such a distinction as you mention. I've certainly never heard of a painter or a powwow practitioner mention this distinction or conflict between the use of blood and paint in the context of traditional motifs. I've heard people say that the red paint represented the blood of Christ, but I've never heard of the question of comparison for efficacy in Hexerei. This is because the vast majority of folklorists, powwow practitioners, and painters I've encountered have never connected the designs specifically to hexerei. They have in many cases connected the designs to healing, dreams, and non-ordinary experiences.

In reference to the question of materials however, I've always assumed that within the philosophy of sympathetic magic, materials which appear to have like qualities are assumed to function in a similar way. I'm also aware that even in the situation of authors like Lee Gandee or Dennis Boyer, both of whom mention specific accounts of the traditional motifs as braucherei tools, it is assumed for both writers that literally everything and anything a braucherin or powwower does has the potential to carry the prayerful intention of the practitioner, whether it is a verbal prayer, a gesture, a written blessing, a ritual wafer, a knotted string, a chalked or painted design, or even common everyday activities such as baking bread or starting vinegar. The materials add content and subtlety, but they are mere vehicles and considered secondary to the intention. I am familiar with the idea of the use of blood for ritual purposes, and often it was used by common, everyday folk and was not considered witchcraft. For instance, several PA Dutch folklorists talk of painting doors of homes or barns with either lamb blood or pig blood for the purpose of protection. Whether this practice was pagan in origin, such as with the swine blood, or biblical in origin by means of the Passover sign, we can't be sure in these syncretic circumstances. I have seen markings on historic buildings that were quite possibly painted in blood, but never any circular geometric designs in blood.

11. What is your interpretation of the PA Germanic usage of the "Fyrfos" or the Hook Cross on their barns?

The whirling-swastika, or Hokegreitz as it was called for some, is one of the oldest designs found on barns and other folk art items. I've never heard Fyrfos used in a PA Dutch context, but rather within the Scandinavian model. Some have called it a Flyfoot in Anglo-Saxon. When I consider the form of a geometric design, whether I know the specific mythology behind it or not, I consider it from a variety of interpretive qualities. The number of radial arms, the orientation of its members, its direction of motion - all have an immediate effect on the viewer and suggest universal certainties. Many of these qualities transcend cultural associations. I think of the Hokegreitz as representing a universal axis, just as an equal-armed cross, whether it is vertically oriented or diagonally oriented, a point of conjunction between equal members. I think of the four members as suggesting the directions of the earthly plane, and the movement as suggesting cyclical motion, perhaps the passage of time. The directional qualities of motion are entirely perceptual. I've experimented with this, and when I ask people which direction a design appears to move, it is usually divided 50/50. Some think of the smaller, rounded edge of the tear drop to lead, others see it as trailing behind. Typically, some historians have dubbed the counter-clockwise motion passive, while the clockwise is active, and this follows the astrological and hermetic notions of polarity. The problem lies in which way the design moves apparently, and this changes from person to person. Many PA Dutch sources have referred to this idea as the Four Seasons, yet I am unable to locate any written or verbal source that actually uses Deitsch terminology for this seasonal idea. I think the historical ideas of this design have been explored ad nauseum by scholars, many of whom had biases because of their wanting a certain culture to claim its point of origination. Some credit Greece, some India, some the pan-continental migrations of "Aryans." I find it all somewhat suspect. Nearly every culture of the world has used the design, and while the PA Dutch may appear to fall distinctly within the Germanic context, it does not necessarily have to relate to the same concepts of Germanic culture which are held by enthusiasts today. Much of what people today believe about Germanic culture is derived from Scandinavian reconstruction and Aryan metahistory. In short, the PA Dutch have been internalizing and creating designs which might fall into a Germanic context, yet they were undoubtedly completely unaware of the history of the Indo-Aryan connection and it did not affect their thinking in the same way it does for Nordo-Germanic enthusiasts today.

The self-awareness of our ancestors was completely different than our awareness of history today.

12. I was told "back in the day" that the droplets between the star rays were called Yods. What is your experience with that term?

I'm curious about the source of this bit of folklore, and how far back in the day this can be traced. It almost certainly references the Hebrew Letter Yod, the first letter of the Tetragrammaton, or the highest unutterable name of God. It fits into a Judeo-Christian context, but it is hard to determine what portion of that context. Many people of today automatically assume anything unusual and Hebrew found in Amero-European culture has a connection with the Hebrew Kaballah, however this has a great deal to do with the popularity of the Kaballah in recent years, and the assumption cannot so easily be made. The problem lies in what the person who mentioned this idea had in mind for the connection between the tear drop and the Yod. The letter carries with it very distinctly Hebrew cultural associations, and it would be difficult to assume that a PA Dutch perspective is entirely compatible. Even when we look to Hebrew words, phrases and ritual practice in undercurrents of PA Dutch mysticism, such as the Feuersegen of Ephrata, the Sixth and Seventh Books of Moses, and the occasional use of the names of God in protective charms and amulets, it is difficult to make generalized assumptions about the intention of the individual using the ideas. My own research has only turned up written references to Hebrew mysticism, and not all of it can specifically be called "Kaballic" on account of a lack of delineation of a cohesive system. There is no evidence to indicate that much of anyone in PA Dutch culture could speak Hebrew fluently, except in the occasional circumstances of theological and scholastic adherents. This is especially the case in a folk scenario, as this knowledge would be incredibly obscure outside the realm of high-education. In many situations, I'm curious whether the person who wrote the charms could read Hebrew at all, or whether the lure of symbols from extra-cultural sources were believed to be inherently powerful because of being unfamiliar and obscure, and therefore were passed down through generations. Even in communities such as Shaefferstown, which was believed to have a substantial number of Jewish inhabitants, there is almost no trace of the population, and some have even questioned, perhaps unfoundedly, whether or not this community ever existed in that location. As for the implications of Yod, we could make assumptions based upon what we know of the concept today, but I feel that this would be a premature assessment. The person who mentioned this to you might know more about the orientation of those who held this connection in common. However, this certainly is an interesting and suggestive bit of folklore, and if your informant gave more specifics, it could potentially be an incredibly valuable piece of information concerning the cross-cultural connections.

13. Of what symbolic significance is the Rossette?

The rosette, like the majority of PA Dutch symbols, is an ancient symbol which has been used extensively in Judeo-Christian and pagan contexts. Some have compared it to the Iota-Chi, the monogram of Christ, while others point to the Hagal rune in later runic alphabets. Both of these connections are inconclusive, as there is circumstantial evidence to suggest that both meanings have had an effect upon the culture that eventually became known as the Pennsylvania Dutch. However, neither of the explanations can be found to have a specific place in Pennsylvania Dutch culture. These are not the explanations of the folk, they are the explanations of the scholastic movements, and few scholars agree. The design has been used extensively in Pennsylvania on Barns, on churches, on tombstones, taufscheins, butter molds, tinware, graffiti, grain sacks, summer sausage bags, ... pretty much everything within the PA Dutch culture that would normally be decorated has been the site of this ubiquitous symbol. I think to understand a folk perspective of the design, we have to think about how the design was made in the plainest of circumstances and why. Farmers used to scribe the designs on mowstead walls with two-tined hayforks used as a compass. The design is created using the inherent properties of the circle as the basis for the geometry. A circle is formed by a continuous line on which every point is equidistant from the origin. These qualities are timeless and have been observed in nearly every culture, and the human reaction to these qualities is predictable: the circle is significant as a symbol for continuity. The circle references both the things we can see with our eyes, as in the sun, the moon and the dome of the heavens, but also things we have to see and interpret with our minds, such as the annual cycle of the year, and the orbits of the stars. These designs reference internalized observations. The rosette is something specific, but it is also universal in this sense.

14. The prevalent attitude coming out of Berks County is that our Hexology is a dying, fading phenomena that needs to be preserved before it is gone completely. The Germanic Heathen community tends to disagree with that assessment. What is your opinion?

I think there is a resurgence in interest in traditional designs throughout Berks County. I've spoken with a large number of people as a result of my research and I'm convinced that the tradition isn't something which will easily pass away, regardless of what name people call it, or how they internalize the designs. I think variation in philosophic orientation is a good thing, it ensures the survival of the traditional designs. The problem lies in the attempt by some to standardize the meanings into something which restricts their living interpretation to a single definition. This has happened to some degree in nearly every fractional group that has wished to lay claim to the iconography, whether the individuals are scholastic, Christian, neo-pagan, commercial, or in the extreme -fascist. Symbols which are distilled by intellectual constraints into a single meaning lose their symbolic qualities, because a symbol is not the same as a word. It cannot be defined by verbal statements, only described. When a symbol can be summed up in a single word or phrase, it becomes a mere sign with a one-dimensional meanings, and it loses its dynamic, universal nature. The survival of these designs depends upon a vested cultural interest in re-investigating, revealing, and re-inventing ourselves.

Interview with Grímnir with Hunter Yoder, 2009

Grimnir and brother, Jarnfr, Sunnewendi, 2010

I have the pleasure today of interviewing Grímnir of the Wolves of Vinland. I heard about him through my der Stamm Mainman, Chris Loscar who was very impressed with the youth, energy, and productiveness of the "Wolves" in general and Grimnir specifically. We met recently at a Sunnawendi celebration in the Pococnos and kept it real. Grimnir also fronts his band, "In Death I Become."

First Question Grimnir:

1. Give us some background about the Wolves of Vinland and how that all happened.

Grimnir: The Wolves of Vinland formed officially when several of our current members relocated to Virginia from Wyoming-several of us had been interested in heathenry, specifically of a radical tribal nature for some time. After the move to Falwell Country, we decided to form a tribally structured heathen community that put more emphasis on Right Action and Right Thought than it did on kindred politics, lore debates and armchair philosophy. Our integrity has been kept up by a long and thorough prospecting period for interested parties, as well as a rigorous work schedule and strict adherence to our tribe's personal Oath. In the past we had been very insular, but recently we have been honored to enjoy partnership with such tribes as the Irminfolk and der Heidevolkstamm.

2. How do you see your musical interests and "the

Wolves" mesh? What things are coming up in the future for the band?

Grimnir: The band and the tribe are definitely separate entities, as half the musical project are not members. However, the general spirit of what we do in the Wolves has been working its way intp the music more and more....our new album, "Black Wings, Grey Skies," set to release in about 2 months time, deals heavily with themes of hamramr, masking ritual, entheogens, and Germanic mysticism. We are also proud to be appearing as a musical guest at the Confederation of Folkish Heathens', Winternights Gathering in October of this year.

3. I know that you have the Nordic blood as well as the Deutsch, how essential is that in practicing an Icelandic version of Heathenry?

Grimnir: I don't know that we, or I, practice a specifically "Icelandic" brand of Heathenry. Some of our members don't have a drop of Scandinavian blood, others are purely German and so forth. Our tribe's name is no accident. We feel that we practice a Vinlandic form of our ancestor's folkway. It has become important to us to study the lore and stay very rooted in the heathen past of our forebears, while at the same time bringing that forward into our current time and place effectively. We also strive to keep our Folk's body of lore a living thing by contributing to it with traditionally styled poetry, prose and so on. The time is definitely now to bridge the gap between our heathen past and heathen present- if we are to keep the tradition alive for the next generation, it is imperative that we make it a thriving and constantly growing thing.

4. We spoke when we met in June about the Appalachian Mountains and how we are joined by them as well as thru our blood. How intense is that relationship? Any experiences from the Mountains you care to share?

Grimnir: The combination is truly a potent one. I hike the Blue Ridge Mts. constantly and have made a lot of friends under the waterfalls there. I often practice galdr and seiðr at falls, as the roaring of the water can either meld with your singing in a powerful fashion, or in the case of seiðr, drown out everything else and act as a catalyst to heightened states. I have learned at great many things from the vætts of the Blue Ridge.

5. It is widely known of your interest in Galdr, but how do you view Seidr?

Grimnir: The two are equally important to me. I have always felt that in order to be fully rounded it was necessary to experience and exercise both. There are many things that galdr cannot achieve that seiðr can and vice versa. Because they are two completely different animals, it is often Needed to completely shift one's perceptions and persona in order to successfully perform an operation with one or the other, and for me this where heiti and hamr come into play.

6. What differences if any do you see between "witchcraft" and "shamanism"? Is it purely semantics?

Grimnir: In my understanding of the two, I would say

that shamanism is generally used more for healing and transcendental/ecstatic states, whereas in the past, "witchcraft" has often had more of a selfish, "profane" sort of slant to it. I also think that shamanism needs a community to function properly. That is, the main purpose of shamanism is for the benefit of a community in most cases, though not always.

7. Since you have the Deutsch blood, do you have any thoughts you care to share about Hexerei?

Grimnir: I have a great deal of respect for the tradition and for those that keep it alive, especially in the form of the hexefoos, etc. I have been interested in hex-signs and so on for a long time, and their relation with galdrastafir/ aegishjalmr; a shared interest that you and I discussed when we met. I am also pleased that there remain folks who approach it in a serious minded fashion, instead of adhering to it's kristjan attributes, or claiming that it never had anything to do with "magic".

8. What are your thoughts regarding trees and the runes?

Grimnir: They are both living growing things that deepen the understanding and wonderment we can have of the natural world, as well as finding our place in it. From seed to mighty oak, so our understanding of Runa- with each new growth, a new opportunity to go ever higher.

9. There is alot of talk these days regarding entheogens. How are these plants and our Northern witchcraft conjoined, if at all?

Grimnir: Entheogens and spirituality/magic have been

linked definitively together nearly everywhere on the planet by anthropologists. Personally I view them as valuable tools to allow us to catch a glimpse outside- once we get a glance there is no going back. It is hoped that one does not become dependent on these tools for spiritual growth or enlightenment, but rather develops his own ability to achieve these states with no helper. That being said, I think there are certain plants that have the ability to change lives in a single use, granting the user the opportunity to shed off his weary way like and old skin- and I count myself as a walking testament of this idea.

10. How are wolves magical animals and which one are you?

Grimnir: The wolf has always been a symbol of Wildness, Freedom, Ferocity and Power. The pack is a perfect microcosm of natural social order and strength through Action, as well as creature of necessity and practicality. In the ongoing struggle for our Folk, and the continued rotting of our modern society, we are in the woods- howling songs of new Growth.

 I'd also like to take a moment to publicly thank a few folks who have been a real inspiration to me in the past few years in one way or another:

Galdr Rölfsson, Gandvaldr Bláskikkja, Chris Loscar, Daniel Nye, Valúlfr Vaerulsson, Hunter Yoder, Thomas Thompson. Each of your Words has led me to another Word, and each Deed to another Deed....

Gandvaldr Bláskikkja Interview with Hunter Yoder

Hunter:

I am delighted to present another great perspective in our ongoing interview series at Zaubereigarten: My well known admiration for the Galdrstaves and their relativity to the Hexerei fueled my interest in interviewing Gandvaldr following the Grimnir interview. Gandvaldr, heads his own rune school, Galdragildi and has written extensively on the Icelandic magical traditions. His "Gandreidr-the Magic Ride" in HEX Magazine issue #4 is included along with my own contribution in the same issue, "Runic Symbology in Contemporary Deitsch Hexology" He has a no nonsense approach to "Neo-shamanism" that speaks to our emerging folkish heathen ways here.

Gandvaldr:

Thank you very much for this opportunity. I've heard and seen good things from you and Zaubereigarten.com and it is an honour to contribute to such a dignified presentation. Though my own approach is far from being that of the core topic of the website, I hope to provide some information and opinion that is of benefit to its readers.

1. What thoughts do you have on oppositional pairings in the Elder Futhark?

I presume the pairings of which you ask are akin to: fehu/dagaz, uruz/othala, thurisaz/ingwaz, and so on. These pairings when looking at the entirety of the Elder row reveals some of the hidden layers of meaning. Given that the runes reflect the pattern of our cosmogony and consciousness, a vitki must understand and use them beyond the obvious stave shapes and general representations intrinsic to their runegaldr. Once these are understood and exercised, capably, one could begin to work with these 'pairings': dyads, and even triads, as they are readily presented to the learned eye, though each works quite different from the other. Probably the most notable and conveniently shared pairing is that which occurs in the very middle of the elder row (or the first dyad, depending on ones chosen course of pairing). It begins with jera and eihwaz: the central runestaves of the Elder fuþark - as the 'milling process'.

2. Seidr and Shamanism, are they more similar then Galdr and Shamanism?

This question requires some discussion because of the sensitivity of the use words like "seið" and "shamanism". I prefer to refrain from generalizing since the term "shaman" and "shamanism" are referring specific practices of Tenguistic culture. Certainly the former has some similarities of approach that could be seen as being shamanistic, but it would be more accurate to compare the practices and traditions to those people inhabiting Sámpi. Rune-galdr is approached quite differently. The ecstatic state that's used for the platform during seið or seið-galdr is not achieved during the course of runic intonation and presentation.

The releasing of the Will into the subconscious would be contraindicated for the functional rune-galdr since focus of the Will needs to be specifically directed into the song / runestave. It's presented within the Hávamál as Óðinn being conscious (ON: *vita*) at key occurrences concerning his own discovery and use of the Runes.

3. Can you speak on attenuation, and multiplication on the rays in the galdrastafir tradition, specifically hatchings (curlycues, cross hatching, squared off on the rays) of various types.

The complexity of the 'rays' and their fields of termination with the overall layout of the galdrastafir, along with galdramyndir, are most easily discussed when presented in *ægishjálmar* (helms of awe) [see fig. 1]. These 'helms of awe' are generally the most recognized forms of galdrastafir, with a central point and radiating branches using the various ends mentioned above for effect. When the galdrastafr / ægishhjálmr is created, the stave is understood to contain fields within the central self, and subjective and objective universes. The specific stave endings are meant to expand, contain, return, amplify or prevent the diffusion of energies within the areas of choice.

Other galdrastafir are composed of bind-runes that may then be stylized to further embed their already hidden meaning and purpose, and increase their aesthetics or to simply make them iconographic as in the various *Þjófastafur* [see figure 2]. Often the only way to dissect the 'meaning' of a particular galdrastafir is to be the vitki who inscribed it, since the stylization and contained intent of the design is often far too complex to accurately define. This is more deeply complicated (and established) by the vocalized or transcribed portion accompanying the process of the galdrastafir, as in the *Nárbrókarstafur* [see fig. 3] for further complexity and *Galdratöluskip* for complexity accompanied by verse [see fig. 4].
(The images are borrowed from the Museum of Icelandic Sorcery web site)

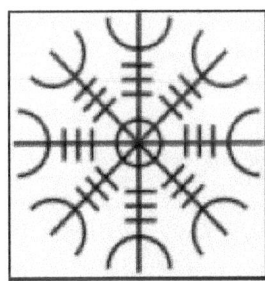
Fig. 1

Fig. 2

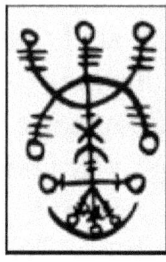

Fig. 3

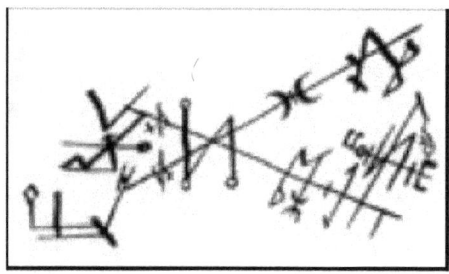

Fig. 4

Hátt eru segl við húna
hengd með strengi snúna.
Séð hef ég ristur rúna
mig rankar við því núna.
Ofan af öllu landi
ógn og stormur standi,
særokið með sandi
sendi þeim erkifjandi.

4. Can you speak on Icelandic witchcraft and usages of Black Henbane?

The use of henbane (*Hyoscyamus niger*) has been a personal favourite for a few years. A trusted friend of mine [Cody] first helped me to understand the particulars of its use some years ago. His knowledge of a wide variety of entheogen is quite inspirational. Since then, I've come to personally work with henbane during various activities and the outcomes have been remarkable. Henbane is one of the notable plants from the nightshade family, Solanaceae, in that it has an extraordinary history of association with witchcraft: necromancy, prophecy, weather magic, in addition to being used for healing, transcendence and spiritual discourse. Use of this for healing is accounted during the black plague as a narcotic salve made from black poplar, poppy, and henbane/deadly nightshade. The concoction was used for a painkiller. This plant was also used in beer-brewing; the last known execution resulting from "brew witches" was in the late 1500s. Today's Pilsner beer has its root in the use of henbane: Pilsnerkraut (and Bilsnerkraut), both German for henbane. It is also said to be of particular use in ending a drought by taking a stalk of henbane, dipping it in a stream and sprinkling the land with its residue. In this along with being brewed into beer is said to be a sacred mixture for the thunder god, as well as an herb of the death-god Odin. Due to its rarity, special gardens were established and dedicated as sacred to the gods Thor and Odin. Some connection, too, has been postulated between the berserkers and use of henbane since its maddening effects are akin to those told of Odin's chosen warriors.

Henbane is, of course, a poison and should never be used, grown or effused when children are near. The entire plant is replete with alkaloids and one only needs to use the leaves mulled into a tea or alcoholic beverage for some result.

5. Black and white magic, is this a purely xtian perspective on Galdra/Hexerei?

I do think this is a *kristinn* judgement placed upon something that, in ones opinion, must be either "black" or "white", "good" or "evil". What I find most curious, is that there are some within the heathen / folkish communities who maintain the same point of view. It's as if the final shackles of *kristinndómr* have yet to be thrown off, much like most persons I've met who practice 'older' religions, or modern wicca. When a person who harms another with a knife or gun, it's not questioned whether the weapon was 'evil', nor whether the weapon had any intent at all. The device was merely wielded by another for their own aims. Even the most globally fearsome of modern weapons, nuclear warheads for example, cannot be seen as 'evil' since without direction and cause, they are at rest - for better or worse. Of course, this in no way implies that magic, Hexerai, rune or seið-galdr, *gandreiðr*, etc. could not be used for dastardly goals, nor that the aforementioned platforms of generation could not create something intrinsically malevolent, as in the Icelandic tales of the *tilberi*, carrier spindles, or sendings, such as *Thorgeir's Bull* (middle 18th c.) that had contained the essence of 9 creatures (including the bull essence) so it could move freely in all areas of land and sky. This dreadful creature was constructed through the combined efforts of several wizards, but only used by Thorgeir. It was initially created to harm Gudrun Bessadóttir for refusing his hand in marriage. However after causing her much discomfort and eventual demise, the Bull turned its attention on others; playing harmful tricks. It seems that the Bull was specifically devoted to Thorgeir. If the Bull couldn't complete a task that its master sent upon it, the Bull would return home and taunt Thorgeir himself. The wizard, though very powerful, had to exhaust all his magic so he may defend against the Bull's attacks. Thorgeir, wanting to be rid of the Bull once and for all, meant to offer his own infant son to it that it may be appeased. His wife persuaded him to provide a heifer instead. This offering was found some distance from the house, shredded to pieces. After this, the Bull appears to have caused no great harm, however it continued to taunt Thorgeir's kinsmen. Thorgeir himself was so afraid of this creature that he made both of his daughters carry runic charms in their aprons for protection. On Thorgier's deathbed, a grey cat (some account a black puppy) lay down upon his chest, and it's presumed to have been the Bull. Thorgier died in 1803, he was 86.

6. Trees, working with wood, why do the runes work

so well with that?

First, I like what Valúlfr has to say regarding a similar question posed to him in his interview. Along with that, I'd like to offer the connection with Yggdrasill, and the All-Father's suspension to win the runes. Taking into account that according to the elder Edda, the gods (Odin-Vili-Ve) first created man from trees – presumably an ash and an elm. The connection a *vitki* or *rúnameistari* maintains in reflection/connection within and without *Yggdrasill* along with the malleable substances with which they work, results in the runes not only being 'risted' into a wood surface, but into themselves as well.

On a practical level, the layered grains of wood when cutting across them hold the staves distinctly apart from the lines of grain. It also provides a natural, available substance with which to work that isn't as unforgiving nor time-consuming as stone might be. When the wood is taken, it is alive and growing: the energies within the wood, or varieties of wood, also lend to the overall result of ones desired work. From the point the wood for the working is procured, to the moment the runes are carved and the tine is 'doomed,' the entire process holds a living thing.

7. Pennsylvania Deitsch Hexerei and the Icelandic Galdr share many commonalities, what is your view from your Icelandic perspective of the PA German magical traditions that have existed continuously since the arrival of the ancestors here?

[Smile] It is more of an Icelandic approach rather than a perspective. The old-world connection to the PA Deitsch magical traditions is rich and impressive. Maintaining a close, strong line over such an expanse of time and distance speaks of its importance. Icelanders, too, are proud of their heritage and culture, but cannot boast of the same transcontinental resilience.

8. In Deitsch Magic we face North in workings, Is this something we share in common and if so why that direction?

It is the same in many of our workings as well. However, from the standpoint of ones goals and intentions for the working process, there are times when facing the East or West (or even South) is in keeping. Some of my own base ritual galdr, for the Nornir, requires attention drawn to the East. Often too, attentions are shifted throughout the working depending on the reflective area of intent. Whichever direction is chosen, this is generally a physical representation of 'from whence' the energies are being drawn or directed.

9. At a time when eclecticism is a naughty word in Heathenism and re constructionist thinking, How eclectic was the Icelandic magic? The impression from the outside is that it is the purest form of Northern European magic.

This depends on the period from which one is drawing their references. The heathen period, before Icelandic conversion, was vibrant and more pure. Given what was transpiring during the pressure to convert to the aims of kristinndómr, there was much crossing over of ideas and techniques; more of a synthesis of both heathen and kristinn. However, due to a lack of written information during this time, there is little actual reference from which to glean. As the Catholic period gave way to the Reformation, and writing became more prevalent, we see the creation of the *galdrabœkur*, magical books that detailed the manner and use of specific practices. Some of the most dreadful magicians throughout the kristinnization and Reformation were those claiming to be religious leaders (kristinn) who were adept with runegaldr and galdrastafir. Beyond this, looking through examples of the "black books" (personal books of folkish magical practices) shows that the folkish magic of the time used both heathen and kristinn methodology as well. It appears to be eclectic and highly adaptive given the pressures of the time and the ongoing development and understanding of transcontinental content. However, these days, there is a desire to remove the dross of the infused kristinn perspectives and re-establish something more akin to what the original Icelanders sought when departing Norway and King Harald fair-haired's goal of a unified kingdom.

Those heathen folk whose practices and interests lie in Germanic magic, vitki, rúnameistari, or seið-kona or maðr, should start at the most 'pure' aspect of the tradition. Once those are truly understood and embodied, which should take years, progression into the complicated synthesis of the Reformation period is a viable and powerful step as long as the wholeness of the tradition and its foundation is upheld.

10. Is ceremonial magic a correct term in describing Icelandic magic after lets say the 1600's?

Tough question... simply saying "yes" or "no" would inaccurately commit my response into an area that is otherwise gray. In some aspects, I suppose it would be thought as such. I prefer to consider it more of a 'ritual magic'* rather than being solely ceremonial. Given the composition of heathen and more contemporary (at any given time) understanding, especially that of kristinn influence, ceremony becomes more prevalent. The various magical books (*galdrabækur*) and other manuscripts of the period depict practices, while complex, do not necessarily fit into the description of ceremonial magic. Germanic magical practices for the long-term student today seem to begin with more of a ceremonial approach, but as experience and knowledge develop, the 'ceremony' gives way to ritual and eventually more informed spontaneity of ones application and use; where dedicate rune or seið galdr and may be permeated with folkish or even sympathetic tools when Needed.

*In my opinion, ceremony is a performance that requires one to practice to flawlessly present it, whereas ritual may permit more free-flowing alteration and variation from one to the other. No two rituals are alike, even when the same foundation is shared.

Troy Wisehart Interview with Hunter Yoder

Today I have the pleasure of talking with Troy Wisehart, a Germanic Heathen who is the leader of the Falcon Kindred based out of Olympia, Washington State. Troy is currently featured in the "Journal of Contemporary Heathen Thought, Volume One " with a beautiful poem entitled, "Baldr's Temple"

Troy Wisehart

Heil Troy, can you give us a synopsis of your personal background, place or places of origin prior to your discovery of Asatru' and the formation of the Falcon Kindred?

Troy Wisehart:

I was born in Arizona in 1962 and lived in that state until my mother moved to Oregon with my sister and I when I was four. At the age of eleven my mother re-married and we all moved to Northern Idaho where I spent most of my teenage years. At fifteen I left on a hitch-hiking excursion to Southern California thinking to live with my father. That did not work out quite like I had envisioned and I ended up back in North Idaho where I finished High School. After graduation I joined the Air Force and went to Germany where I discovered real beer as well as other European pleasures.

In 1984 I separated from the Air Force with an honorable discharge and returned to Idaho where I worked as a laborer for my step-father's masonry company. I eventually migrated back to Arizona where I met Dave Taggart and discovered Asatru. It was there in Mesa at a house on Raven St. that Falcon Kindred was founded. In 2005 I relocated to the Pacific Northwest where I currently reside in the Olympia area of Western Washington State.

Hunter Yoder:

There is a trend amongst the Folk to take on the study of

the Runes, why do you suppose that is? Any thoughts on joining a Rune School or Rune Schools in general? Many, or most Folk take up the study of the Runes...do you think this is for everyone? Should there be degrees of knowledge?

Troy Wisehart

In my experience, the runes are of great interest to most people who end up embracing the religion of their ancestors. I believe this is because the minni within us recognizes the runes on a subconscious level and we are instinctively drawn to them. The runes call to us. We somehow know that there is information to be got through them that is available nowhere else. Once we hear the call our thirst for knowledge is never quenched and so we inquire and search.

Rune schools can be valuable learning tools. I think it is wise to seek out those with more knowledge and experience. I try to make a point of associating with people who know more than I do. They challenge me and offer me perspectives that I might not have considered otherwise. For now however I am content to continue with my current course of runic study and meditation on my own. Falcon Kindred often has a runic discussion at our events. Even though I lead those sessions I end up learning something from everyone there. The perspective of others is always very interesting. I also have conversations with several of my friends who study the runes. But I find that reading and talking are only part of the runic journey. The most important element for me is the time I spend alone singing the galdr of the runes and meditating on those energies. Once the mind has been cleared of mental clutter and the way has been opened to the abyss connection to the runes might be established. That is when the "knowing" becomes.

There are degrees of knowledge with the runes to be sure. Those degrees can be earned and bestowed in a structured curriculum or a person can simply study on their own. Just like any other form of knowledge, there will some who are further down the road than others. It is a journey that cannot be hurried. The information will come when it does and only if fervently sought. We must persistently seek it. It requires dedication. It is not for everyone.

Hunter Yoder:

I recall engaging in an online thread with you regarding animal sacrifice which I suppose is a controversial subject fraught with emotion, but my interest in bringing it up is nonjudgmental. Animal sacrifice is very ancient and is common among all ancient cultures. What is the basic mechanism at play in this rite between the gods and goddesses, the folk and the sacrifice?

Troy Wisehart:

The basic mechanism at play between the gods, the folk, and the sacrificial animal is the shared energy of life. In all things there is Sol. It is released upon the death of the lyke. It is my belief that the Sol resides in the blood. Our ancestors knew this and that is why they offered blood sacrifice. For the gods and goddesses that energy is received when the blood is caught in the bowli and offered on the horg. The Folk are besprinkled with the blood and receive a portion of that energy as well. Then at feast the first and best is set aside and offered to the god or goddess through fire. The sustenance got by consuming the flesh of the blot animal is pure and sacred.

There is still more at play here though. It is not an easy thing to raise an animal. A place must be prepared to keep the animal and it must be cared for every day. For city dwellers it is even more of a challenge because they are not able to keep livestock in town. The logistics get pretty complex. But all that preparation and dedication are as much a part of the offering as the ritual slaughter itself. The gods and goddesses are aware of our actions when it comes to these activities and at times will even assist. A coincidental acquaintance who just happens to have just what you need or a friend dropping by right when you need a hand. Little things, and big things too, that let you know you are not in it alone. The gods and goddesses have a way of blessing us in advance. When we say we are going to do a thing we are taken at our word and treated as if it is already done. It is very important that we follow through!

Hunter Yoder:

I really enjoy the Falcon Kindred's Galdrstafir as you

recently explained to me, "The bind rune is Fehu/Kenaz X 8. Falcon Kindred. (8 X 1)+(8X6)=56 or ISA. Fehu= fire, Kenaz = fire, Isa = ice. Fire and ice = creation " What connection if any does something like that have with the Deitsch Hexology. What are your thoughts on using runes and bindrunes on the Hexology?

Troy Wisehart:

To me all these symbols serve the same purpose. They are focal points for the mind of the magician. The runes are keys to the energies of the multi-verse. With them we are able to emulate our gods and divine or affect ourselves and things outside ourselves. The stave shapes of the runes are indicative of their function and the body of lore surrounding them teaches us how best we might employ them for specific purpose. The galdr staves are a type of map for the mind to extend its influence out into the multiverse through conscious act of will. And the Hex's combine various symbols to bring about the desired effect. It makes perfect sense that these three types of magical symbols would naturally work well in combination. They are all Germanic in origin so nothing would be in conflict. It is the will of the magician expressed skillfully in formali that activates any and all of these magical symbols.

Hunter Yoder:

I see from your description in the contributors section of the 'Journal' Volume One that you cite Freyja as the

Goddess who took you and Dave Taggart under her wing in the formation of your Falcon Kindred. What can you say about that and how has that relationship with Freya evolved?

Troy Wisehart:

When Dave and I first became involved in Asatru we immediately understood that we were to form a kindred. It was simply a matter of fact. We had been reading and discussing things for several months back in 1999 and had decided to do a blot on Halloween. For some reason it was not clear to us what god or goddess should receive the offering and so we contemplated and considered but remained unsure. Then one evening as we sat in the living room attempting to choose the right deity we heard a meowing outside our front door. It was a pure black male kitten on our door step and it became apparent at that point that Freya had provided the answer for us. And so it was that Falcon Kindred's first ever blot was to the Queen of the Vanir.

Hunter Yoder:

We both share a love for the 'Black Sun' symbol. I've used it in the Hexology as the metaphorical sun that shines for those of Germanic descent, a symbol that is found in the artifacts of the Alemani tribe, 500CE. I have seen it as a Sonne Rod or sun wheel and as the wagon wheel, symbolizing the great migration period of our ancestors. What is your take on this powerful wheel?

"Ein prosit auf unserer schwarzen sonne, seinem weissem licht und unserem roten blut!"

Der Heidevolksstamm

Troy Wisehart:

I have always been drawn to the symbol of the Black Sun. However, I actually know very little about it. My initial investigations through internet searches have brought me mostly Satanic associations but I flatly reject that information as irrelevant for my purposes as a Germanic magician. Of course there are the wretched Nazis and their usurpation of this as well as many other sacred Germanic symbols. We see what the misuse of our holy signs brought that lot. Most of what I think about the Black Sun is subjective. Naturally I see the twelve Sowilo runes as the rays of Sunna. The number twelve is the number of Jera and also of months in the year so the seasons are represented by this symbol as well. But what I mostly feel is that the Black Sun is Mani. It is somehow associated with lunar eclipses as Sunna herself would appear to be black during this event. I like to imagine that in the proper state of mind witnessing an eclipse would be like looking into the eye of Odin. Eclipses have traditionally been powerful times of ritual and so if indeed the Black Sun has something to do with Mani blocking out Sunna it would validate my theory. Perhaps the alignment of Sunna and Mani create some type of gate way. It even seems pro-creational in some way. I can only speculate and at this point it is only my personal theory.

Here's to our black sun, its white light, and our red blood! "The pagan tribe."

Hunter Yoder:

I have a friend here in Philadelphia, 'on the block' so to speak. He asks me why Donar's hammer is worn by Odinists? Furthermore he asks me why is it worn upside down? On that I suggest that its purely a matter of gravity and tradition. On the former, I suggest that Donar is the far older God, the God of Thunder, Odin or Wotan a relatively recent addition. What are your thoughts?

Troy Wisehart:

Thor's hammer is the best known symbol of Germanic Heathenry. If someone were to be interested in advertising their religion for whatever reason wearing the hammer of Thor would be the easiest way to do it. It is also regarded as a mighty protective talisman and many may feel that they are warded when they wear it. I always enjoy seeing a hammer around someone's neck although I seldom wear one myself except for special occasions like ritual. Personally I prefer to keep my religious views to myself. At one time I was pretty militant about being an Asatruar and felt the need to make sure everyone knew that I was a Heathen. But for some reason as I have gone further and further down the Odian path I feel less and less compelled to show anyone anything outside of my own kindred. I feel perfectly comfortable with what I am and certainly have no need for a talisman to feel protected. My protection comes from being allied and aligned with my wyrd and the holy powers.

Hunter Yoder:

In your poem 'Baldr's Temple' Baldr is reborn or reemerges from Hel anew. This is a very old theme in the Germanic mythologies. Von List describes the Fanisk or Phoenix reemerging from the ashes of the Ar or Urfyr or the placing of fertility cult objects in burial sites. What is your personal take on this and on how many levels does it operate? Would it be mistaken to interpret your poem as a personal transformative process in our own lives today?

Troy Wisehart:

Actually "Baldr's Temple" is inspired by the Norwegian shamanic band Wardruna. After watching a series of Youtube videos entitled "True Norwegian Black Metal" in which Gaahl explained that the music was a spell to bring Baldr back from Hel I became fascinated with the concept. The poem "Baldr's Temple" is the result of that fascination. I have given it some thought as to what it would mean if Baldr did indeed return from Hel. If Baldr were to return from Hel it would mean the prophesy of Voluspa had been fulfilled and Ragnarok had begun. It would be the beginning of the next cycle of being. Let us hope Warduna's spells are successful!

Hunter Yoder:

There seems to be a great deal of those of Deutsch descent in the Great North West. How Nordic should the Heathenry of those Folk be? Is it time for those of German descent to step up to the plate and be publicly proud of their origins? I foresee a time in the very near future when practicing a Continental German form of Neopaganism will no longer be a stigma in the Asatru' community. How do you see that?

Troy Wisehart:

I have never personally encountered any stigma associated with being German in the Heathen community. But then I am mostly limited to internet contact with other Heathens and the members of Falcon Kindred. We are a fairly close knit group and have found it prudent to be very selective about with whom we associate. We have a criteria that people must meet before they are even considered for participation in our events. When faced with this most do not contact us a second time.

Although I do know that there are some differences in the practice of our religion between the Scandinavians and the Germans those differences are minimal. I am not able to speak with authority on this topic however because I have almost exclusively pursued the more Nordic route. It seems to be working for me.

Hunter Yoder:

You and your kindred are very busy with your ministry in the prison system. What can you tell us about that? Any Hexology classes?

Troy Wisehart:

Falcon Kindred is no longer active in prison ministry. To begin with I was the only one that was doing this ministry but I arranged for several other members of the kindred to go through the orientation and back ground check required to participate. At one point we were able to distribute the prison visits between five of us. With that many volunteers it really was not much of an inconvenience to go to the prison once every few months or so. But then all but me and Godi Herigstad were available to minister at the prisons and it became too much. In addition, the kindred is involved in other projects that we feel are more worthy of our time and resources. Several prisons have contacted me requesting that I sponsor the Asatruar in their facilities but I simply do not have the inclination.

Orva Gaile Clubb nee Price Interview with Hunter Yoder

Heil Orva,

As I sit here now at the HEX FACTORY sipping a inexpensive California Cabernet Sauvignon and nibbling on some Cortes Chocolate from Puerto Rico I thought I would ask a very good friend of mine, Orva Gaile Clubb some tough questions because of her well known knowledge in 'folk magic' Orva who now lives in Key West Florida originates from rural Southern Maryland and was raised in the old ways Johnny Ott calls the Jinks or Hexerie, the high German name is Hexerei. I met Orva in a Yahoo group called Hexenkunst, it became very clear immediately that she was the 'real McCoy' and had been raised on the farm as myself. Her experience in Rural Maryland mirrored my own in Berks County near Virginville. Direct childhood experiences of this kind trump any other forms of knowledge most especially those derived from the internet.

<u>ORVA</u>

1. Hey Orva, tell us the where and when of your childhood upbringings.

Hi Hunter… Thank you for inviting me for this interview. I think I will start with where I was born and go from there! I was born in Washington DC on July 24, 1949 on Capitol Hill. I was raised with my Mother's parents because my Mother took a job working with the State Department typing classified material from WWII and was sent to Paris, France shortly after I was born. My father was drafted and sent to Korea.

My grandparents along with myself moved out of DC to Southern Maryland when I was quite young, I think around 2 years old or so. We lived in a little one room house my Grandfather Pap built, and lived there without electricity or indoor plumbing or running water until I was in the second grade when we added onto it. It was a very rural setting, and we were surrounded by woods and nature and we raised a few farm animals. Both of my Mother's parents were from Pennsylvania and our family clan was based in Bedford/ Blair Counties located up on the Ridges. Prior to that, many of my folk migrated from Berks/ York and Lancaster counties by way of the "Ridges". Ever since I could remember as a child, we would travel back to that area in the Ridges to visit with family and attend gatherings. After arriving one of the most important things that we did was to visit our dearly departed. So, I went along and trudged to every family cemetery in both counties and was told stories about each and every one who resided there, and believe me there were plenty to go around. Of course each had their own story to tell alive and dead. That is how I learned a lot of our family oral history… for instance that my Grandmother's Great Uncle Frank had three sets of teeth. He was born with a set of teeth already in place, when he lost them he got his milk teeth or baby teeth and finally his adult teeth. He was a huge man in statute and quite famous for his ability to grow teeth!!! Every time we would stand by his grave site those words would be summoned up as a memorial to him, and the words still ring in my ears to this very day.

Every year we would go back "UP HOME" to Pennsylvania, which was how my Grandparents would refer to our visits. There is where both sides of their families lived and we would have large family gatherings. One such large gathering we attended was referred to as the "Corn Boil" or harvest feast held on August 1st of every year. That is where and when all the "old timers" family and extended family would get together at my grandmother's sisters home. Here is where the men folk would smoke or chew tobacco and tell their "stories" while the women would do the cooking and tell their own stories. There was always food cooking and lots to eat, of course corn was the main focus. We had all the traditional dishes and then we would all make homemade peach ice-cream out of fresh milk from the local cows.   I was mostly sent to sit with the men, which was quite unusual for the time… First because I was a child and second because I was a girl child. I was, however, under the protection of my grandfather, so I was accepted as long as I was good and didn't talk. My grandfather's given name was Orva and his family nickname from birth was **Jinx**. I was named Orva after him, and my maiden name was Price/ Welsh Pryce. My father came from old Welsh family blood who were some of the first families of Virginia; however, after I was named in honor of my grandfather, Pap, I also ended up with his nickname, mine as **Jinxie** or **Little Jinx**. And from what I am told we both well-earned our nicknames.

I was well loved as a child and learned things at an early age, however, some of the things I was taught most adults, much less children my age, were not introduced to. These things were different and outsiders would not understand what they were, much less what they meant, or what or how they were used. So I was taught to never talk of these things outside of our family.

I learned to read and write before I went to school, but differently from the rest of the kids. I learned to write in cursive script like how they wrote at the turn of the century and I learned to read from the Newspaper. Consequently, when it came to "Run Spot Run", I was at a complete loss. To print the alphabet was like Chinese to me. I had to learn all these things all over again as a first grader in a mainstream Elementary School in 1955. Also, some activities that we practiced at home would have become somewhat difficult to explain, as I was raised with the mindset of adults who were born at the turn of the century, so what we did at home, stayed at home.

Some of my earliest memories were the Holidays. We had a Yule log and a pine tree we would cut and put up in the house and decorate with homemade ornaments made of pine cones and such, but there was never a Nativity scene ever present. At Easter we celebrated the fullness of new growth and fertility, but the crucifixion of the passion of Christ was never a part of our family tradition. We would hunt for Easter Eggs and find our

Easter baskets and then Pap would usually give me a new baby bunny and or live peep peeps so I could care for as pets. The rest of the livestock was off limits and reserved for food. Killing and butchering, skinning and rendering were a normal natural thing and process in my childhood household. Nothing was wasted; lard was used for cooking and also turned into soap and salves. Rabbit hides were stretched and cured and made into soft winter wear or turned into rabbit hide glue. Taking off warts using a potato was common place. Finding water in underground sources is something my Pap could do. He was taught that process on the ridges, so when we moved to Maryland he could walk the land and find underground springs and then mark the place to dig a well. He did use a rod, mostly in a Y shape or something that looked like a very large turkey wish bone. I would walk the ground over and pace it off with him and he would show me the spot as to where it was good to dig.

My life had a different beat and rhythm to it. Things we practiced that were common place were not ever found outside of our home, so some things I figured were just best left at home quiet like. The Ozzie and Harriett households of the world back then just wouldn't "Get It"

My Grandmother (Mom) was brought up as a Dunkard and many of our folks on her side were Brethren, Mennonite. My Grandmother was a great believer in Sunday school. Every Sunday I attended the Free Methodist Church with Sister Fredrick and Sister Kelly leading the flock to salvation complete with hells fire and damnation written in brimstone. I loved hearing that ole time preaching and going to Sunday school and singing the old hymns. Mom gave me a quarter to put into the offering plate * big money at that time*, and I would dutifully place the quarter into the plate and make change and take out a dime and a nickel. My Pap would drive me to Sunday school in our '36 Plymouth (with run boards on the sides) to make sure I got there on time. But I was left to walk home afterward in case I wanted to stay after tor cookies and cool aide. Knowing me, of course, when the service was over I ran across the street to the local Country Store where slot machines and pin ball machines were set up. The rule was if you could reach the handle of the slot machine you were old enough to play… But you could always find a coco cola box or two to stand on in case you ran a little short. So I had a nickel to play the slots and one to play pin ball and enough left over to buy some penny candy. When I came home Mom was always at the old Hoosier cabinet wearing her apron, dusted full of flour, and had the radio dial set to gospel music and would be just a singing "Rock of Ages" at the top of her voice as she rolled out pot pie egg noodles.

When I finally meandered back home, she would ask me how Sunday school went so I told her about the hymns we sang, and how Sister Frederick and Sister Kelly would shake rattle and roll come sermon time. She asked me if I put my quarter in the plate and I said "Yes Momma" and that was that. She was happy and LIFE WAS GOOD complete with baked chicken Pot Pie and biscuits for supper, fresh out of the old cook stove.

<u>Age 5</u>

Mom often would make her own sauerkraut and homemade ale. I remember hearing her tell that once when she put the crocks of cabbage under the porch to ferment, they actually blew some of the boards loose from their nails. She once made some homemade ginger ale and capped it and stored it under our bed (back then I often shared a bed with my cousin) we got to jumping on the bed one day and next thing we knew, pop pop pop, all the caps started to popping off the bottles. Mom was mad as a wet hen and I remember getting a real licking with a switch for being so "rambunchous". The ale was a real mess to clean up, it was smelly and sticky and it went everywhere, but it was fun jumping on the bed just the same, even knowing that such activity was not allowed. The licking wasn't so bad, but I can remember others that were more severe. She could draw whelps over my legs if she got really worked up enough steam using thin stitches she would cut from a tree sapling. I usually tried to seek Pap's protection, but sometimes he would be at work and I had to take it standing up. I never cried and that made her even madder. As soon as I was let loose I high tailed it to the woods to lick my wounds. There I found peace and comfort. When I came home a nice hot meal was waiting for me and my grandmother was there with open arms. She didn't understand my nature as a kid like my Pap and Aunt Elda did, sometimes I vexed her to the point that she was at a loss as to what to do with me. She used to say I acted like a "wild Injun" which she was not too far off the mark because I have Native American blood on my father's side. I was head strong and punishment didn't seem to work, so after a while I was just left to do things my way. I was a pretty good kid growing up; I had a lot of imagination and was very inquisitive. Now of days they call it thinking out of the box. I hated school and found the creek much more educational so when I got the chance I would head down to the woods and follow the creek and go exploring. My Pap said what made me so smart was I could think both frontwards and backwards at the same time.

The stories that I was brought up on were amazing to me and I was fascinated by the deeds my elder folks did and how they lived and how they were connected to me. As I grew older it all began to come together and I was able to weave it all into a unique family tapestry to pass down to my children and grandchildren. Later in life as an adult I became the manager to my husband's family cemetery in Maryland were we have 6 generations of his people laid to rest. I guess family history has always been important to me and I had a knack for it so becoming an Archivist and Historian and a Professional Genealogist came naturally to me. I was employed by the National Society of the Daughters of the American Revolution (DAR) for 10 years as a Senior Staff Genealogist and was a spoke person for then at National Genealogical Conferences and also helped write and teach a DAR training course to help new genealogists interpret records and find their family trees. But my heart is still in the Ridges and with those long gone kinfolk who taught me my first lessons of life.

My Grandparents: My Pap and Mom

2 .I know your Pap was a big influence what can you share with us about him?

My Pap was born in 1894 on the Ridges of Blair Co., Pa. He was a WWI Veteran and spent 3 years on the front line fighting in the trenches in France, armed with mustard gas masks and a gun and bayonet. He lived those 3 years in a "Pup" tent and ate "hard tack". When he left his home he had a full head of dark hair, but when he returned and married my Grandmother, his hair had turned completely White. He was a very brave and a remarkable man and one that has left an ever lasting imprint on me that help mold me into who I am today.

He was born one of a set of twins. Before I was born he knew I was going to be a girl, he could predict the sex of babies before they were born,(one of the many gifts that has been passed to me.) He had what they now call "the sight" but he could tell things ahead of time what was going to happen, he knew that he and my grandmother would raise me. As a child I bonded with my Pap right away and was sort of his "side kick". We would do projects together in his workshop, I remember one of the first projects was making a Yule Log… we had great fun putting it all together and then crowning it with a deer stag on top. By the time I was done I had swollen fingers from hitting them with a hammer trying to drive horseshoe nails into the wood to hold down the greenery, and I was covered from head to toe with shellac… needless to say, my grandmother was not happy with either of us. I was scrubbed with turpentine till I thought I wouldn't have any skin left.

Once we were in his work shop and he was using a power saw that ran off of gasoline. He came too close and cut off the end of his thumb. I saw all the blood and his left over finger lying on the saw. He calmly asked me to get him a clean shop rag from the bin and he then wiped off his thumb the best he could and then stuck it down inside a can of axel grease and wrapped it with black electoral tape. After his doctoring was done he went inside and set on his rocking chair and took out some tobacco and had a good smoke. His thumb healed up fine, later he dressed it with bear grease and tape and would chew tobacco and spit unto wound before he dressed it. We had different greases for different medical uses; they were all mixed at home by Pap. Some had sulfur in them that turned them yellow, some were green??? Your guess is as good as mine. All of our cuts and scrapes they were usually tended to with a smearing of grease and a Band-Aid or wrapping. He would recommend eating a raw onion for good measure, along with a good measure of horseradish and Black Strap molasses (not all at the same time) to keep the blood up to fight off infection.

In the Spring on May 15th, I was allowed to shed my winter undershirt and go barefooted. In preparation to this monumental event a good healthy dose of Black Strap molasses was administered. In the Wintertime I was administered Creosote Emulsion at the first sign of a cough.

I cut my baby teeth on bacon rind and had whiskey

rubbed on my gums to ease the pain. When my baby teeth got loose I was sent out to him in his work shop where he would get out his needle nosed pair of plyers and pull it out. No tooth fairy ever came to my house, but my teeth were kept hidden away in a cup in the cupboard. I found them all after my grandmother died. Hair and teeth had magical powers so they were treated with special care. I was sent to bed with a clove packing and a piece of rock candy on a string that came from a bottle of Rock and Rye.

I often got things stuck in my hair that had to have it cut out, so I sported a lopsided Dutch Boy hair cut most of the time until I was old enough to wear long curls, (something the Devil must have invented for girls to endure). But at the time of my bob haircut, my knees and shins were mostly covered with scabs and bruises due to my total dedication and insistence that I could fly. !!! I would leap off of the porch roof at home and out of trees and anything that I thought would give me a good "lift", even mounting the rafters in the house only to find myself spread out on the wooden floor with a fine loud thump. I was persistent until finally I gave up that notion after 2 years of failed attempts at the age of 7. My Pap tended to me and would splint my broken fingers with Popsicle sticks and encouraged me that one day I would meet my calling but flying freestyle was not amongst it.

He tended to all my wounds from torn extracting things from my feet and stone bruises from going barefooted in the woods to splinters that festered. He knew all the remedies and could "fix" them when I needed them cured. Hs had salves for soothing and salves to draw out poison. He always seemed to know just what needed to be done and how to do it. His knowledge was valuable and limitless.

Now of days Parents would be locked up and kids put into protective services by the standards we kids of the '50's were raised. After moving to Maryland I can remember that there were 2 cloths lines that where strung between the Oaks. One was for the family needs, and the other was for ME. I had a nice little softly padded harness strapped around me and then hooked onto the close line so I could run and play outdoors without straying off into the wild world beyond. I remember right after I escaped the cloths line that we had a little goat that was brought into our fold… soon there afterwards the goat ate all the cloths off of the cloths line Mom had just hung out… the goat didn't last long after that, I'm not sure what happened to it… (Don't ask/ don't tell) but all I know is both us KIDS were set free. No more cloths lines for us.

Me, having Pennsylvania German along with some Welsh blood with a touch of "Injun" running through my veins, I found after my harness days were put aside, they erected and put me into a 6 foot enclosed fence thinking that would keep me out of trouble, it didn't take me long to figured out how to scale it and escape enabling me to go about MY OWN business, which was mostly playing in the mud or trying to give the cat a bath (not one of my better ideas) and going down to the creek to catch tad poles. I found out what poison ivy was real quick. Another lesson in torture, the cure was worse than the cause. I was stripped naked and had cooled boiled milkweed poured all over me from head to toe. I must have made 50 laps around the picnic table before the fire finally faded from my skin. After 3 days of treatment it was all gone and I remembered thereafter to walk a wide circle around the stuff.

Mom would tolerate my doings most of the time, but she drew a line when I came home smelling like I had fallen down inside the outhouse, (which I did accidently one time when my cousin thought it would be fun to lock me in with the spiders) so on those occasions she would strip me down first then hose me off and scrub me good with Packard's Black Tar Soap till I was raw and squeaky clean. In the summer we were bathed outside in a big wash tub. Since I was the littlest I got in first, then my cousin and finally the dog. It was a grand time for us because we all got wet and ran around naked and laughed till we all got silly. Pap would draw the water from the well and Mom would heat it over the coal burning wood cook stove. Afterwards we would wait up at night and catch lightening bugs and put them in a ball jar for a night light. This was a special treat, because we only had coal oil burning lamps that were put out at night with only the light from the stars as night lights.

However, the real lessons I was being taught was by my Pap you would not find in any book or school. He taught me about Dreams and how to interpret them and read them. At the same time he was teaching me the meanings of shapes and colors in dreams, he also showed me the "backdoor" out of a dream in case I needed to escape. I continued to apply the same principal my entire life, and use it even to this day. I always have an alternative plan working somewhere in my background where there is "My Backdoor." My escape hatch and safe place.

He taught me about fire and how to read events or happenings in the flames. He would tell me to look into the Blue, the Blue runs True. He carried much wisdom about animals and why those that were pets were different than those that were to be slaughtered and eaten, their habits, why some hibernated and why some didn't, and each their own magical significance. He carried so much wisdom about so many things it is difficult to relay the true lesson by just writing it down, I had to feel them as well as learn them. He taught me how to make remedies and administer them, most importantly; he introduced me to the world of Pennsylvania Folk Magic and how our people survived living on the Ridges.

My Pap's twin sister was named Elda. Elda was a lot like my Pap; she was a strong outspoken woman and quick minded and straight to the point. She did not mince her words when she had something to say. I spent a lot of time with her when we went to Pa. She knew the old ways and also the ways and things that women were taught to women only by women. She was somewhat of a Mid-wife and had knowledge in that area. She was good at burns and cuts and could heal them rapidly without infection setting in. She could stop blood during childbirth which saved many women's and babies lives at the time. She knew how to turn a baby without getting the cord all tangled up or how to grab its feet to free it from its mother's womb. To bring a baby on she would use mustard seed plasters, to stop the blood she had many ways, one was to use Fire and Ice. Hot and Cold. My Aunt Elda did not see me as a little girl who was full of mischief and hard headed, but saw something in me that was unique and treated me not as a child but as an equal. We were kindred spirits; she was the other side and duel part of my Pap.

Trouble always seemed to gravitate towards me, but my Pap and my Aunt Elda were there for me and understood me as no one else was able to. They were whole and real. Elda was also richly steeped in the folk ways and culture that was passed down to her from many generations; Wisdom as well as Insight with the natural ability of Knowing.

3. We have discussed 'walking the ridge' what is that?

"The Ridges" were very special, but not withholding from danger. My people found them as passage ways going back and forth across land instead of up and down from North to South and back again. Since the first one of my Pennsylvania ancestors set foot onto this new land they instinctively sought out the Ridges, walking them from East to West and back again from West to East.

There are many places that, for lack of a better definition, held magic in certain areas. There were unusual sightings of unworldly creatures that lived on the ridges and children and babies had to be protected from them for fear of being stolen or exchanged for one of their kind. Quite often a stag would be brought down from off the Ridges and kept to be slaughtered later. I remember seeing such stags being fed and held, hidden away in barns or sheds, to be kept and slaughtered on special occasions. The reason for this runs deep in our tradition and was never spoken about. The ridges were a place where men went to earn their lively hood as woodsmen (lumberjacks). My grandmother's father was such a man and stories were told of his experiences of the magical places and creatures he would encounter. Charms were put around babies cribs such as iron and under their mattresses to ward off evil spirits that also dwelled on the Ridges. Whispered lullaby's (chants) were often used and little pieces of paper tied or pinned to underclothing as prayers would be offered to counteract any ill doing to avoid the Evil Eye. I wore a belly band around my navel with a silver dollar sewn into that included a prayer for safety, to ward off childhood diseases and other such horrors of the day. The belly button or navel was considered a direct network to your soul in children and until it healed it needed to be covered and protected; especially from something that came off the Ridges. When my children were born they also wore belly bands!! Old habits die hard and folk lore and some folk medicine even harder. In Spite of all the lore that I heard about the Ridges they held a very important role in my ancestors lives. The Ridges are magical and wondrous and beautiful and my people made their livelihood from them as well as a passageway to travel from place to place. The Ridges hold secrets like singing rocks and ice caves and fresh water that bubbles up from deep within the earth, some hot and come cold. The Ridges were the heart and soul of my ancestors; they walked them and made their homes in them, and stored within them their stories, history and lore. Our deep rooted heritage and culture lays imbedded within every rock and stream and tree within their terrain.

4. *Give us your views on the plants, I know you have an aversion for parsley, and that tobacco was something you were brought up with and used magically.*

In my childhood home as well my current home as an adult, Parsley was and still is considered a taboo. We did not grow it or use it in cooking or any other way. It was considered to be the funeral flower and it was never ever grown or used. Our meals were strictly Pa. Dutch traditional cooking. I was a grown woman before I ever tasted spaghetti. Any food that was not of our Pa. Dutch culture was considered foreign food and only foreigners ate it. Needless to say anyone who was not of Pa. Dutch heritage was considered outsiders. We were very clannish and kept to ourselves at a polite distance.

Tobacco: Southern Maryland was very rural. We did not

live far from where Dr. Mudd lived (he fixed John Wilkes Booth's broken leg and was sent to prison for it; and Mary Surratt's tavern. She was the first woman to be hung by the federal government for the crime of conspiring to kill Lincoln) Farming and Plantations in the early days of Maryland's history were common place. One of the main crops that were grown there was Tobacco.

My Pap learned to chew and smoke tobacco as a child by his mother who lived on the Ridges in Pa. Tobacco was a very important substance to them for various reasons, and one of the most important ones was for healing and for folk magic. Living in So. Md. It was very easy to come by good grade tobacco for chewing and smoking and it was plentiful. We grew tobacco in our home gardens for good luck and as a pesticide. A hand of dried tobacco hung from the rafters in the home would keep us safe from any form of petulance.

As a child I had sore throats a lot as well as severe ear aches. I was given horehound to suck on and some watered down rock and rye to sip on. When I got feverous my Pap would tie a red wool string *yarn* around my neck with a knot and then sing a lullaby over me. He called his singing "diddies", but they were actually chants to draw out the ill humors. He would gather me into his lap and rock me on the same rocking chair he was rocked in when he was a child. After a while he would take a smoke (hand rolled cigarette) and blow smoke into my infected ear. Then he would take a chaw of tobacco and chew it then spit it in the coal bucket beside the cook stove, and gently lift me to bed after I became restful and had fallen to sleep in his arms. The ear ache finally went away within a few days, my fever broke and I was up and at it again. However, as a side line he taught me how to roll my own smokes by hand and by the time I was 5, I was chewing small chaws of tobacco to spit in the coal bucket. But that use only happened on special occasions.

During those times of illness I can remember him holding me on his lap, my head against his chest while he sang to me and blew smoke in my ear and rocked me. I still remember his strong arms around me and the smell of him. He smelled so very good to me; it was a mixture of wool and clean soap and his strength: A Man's smell that I later learned in life, when I married my husband, He had the same smell about him; Clean and very manly; The smell of mature Manhood just below the surface and of well-earned sweat that had a sweet aroma that lingered like musk. As an adult it was extremely intoxicating to me. As a child it was my security.

In my home we also employed the use of "Diddy Bags" known as Asafceitida or Asafetidy . They were little pouches made of this foul smelling herb that was worn under you underclothing. Many a day I went to school smelling like dung pile due to this herb to keep all forms of EVIL away. I had little prayers or Himmelbrief's pinned to my undershirt or tucked inside my "diddy" bag to make sure I was kept safe from the creatures who walked by day and night or the "Communists"… in the

1950's we believed they were EVERYWHERE !!!!

5. Snakes and salt, I know you fear the one and use the other, what can you share with us about that?

I hate snakes… the only good snake is a dead one! I know now of days snakes are considered to be helpful and some even eco- friendly. They were important symbols in ancient times. However, that is not my mindset. Growing up in my childhood home and throughout my whole life into adulthood, I still adhere to what was taught to me as a kid. I grew up in the woods and we always kept an ax beside the door so if they would get in the house, which they often sometimes did, they were swiftly delivered with a good whack. My grandmother could smell out a snake in a heartbeat and wheel that ax like greased lightning. I keep an ax by my door just in case one comes a calling, and am not afraid to use it. Now that I live on an Island outside of Key West, I keep an ax and a machete next to my door. Living here is like living in Jurassic Park !! At night we can hear the herd of 6 foot long iguana's running across the roof, which is just one of an assortment of other critters that find the tropics suitable to make their home.

Now about the Salt: During the first of May (breeding season for snakes so I was told) my Pap would "ring the house with salt" to keep the snakes away. Snakes don't like salt and will stop dead in their tracks if they come up against it when put down right. To lay it down right you need a chant (I use the one out of the Book of Psalms) and then walk completely around the house putting it down around the foundation. Also extra salt was put at each threshold and entrance of the house to keep dis-ease and other unwanted invasive maladies to enter. Hag riding would also fall into this category... but you need metal for that too. But that is a whole different topic all in its self....

6. You are an expert in programming crystals, What exactly are we talking about here?

I would not consider myself an expert.... But I have been working with them and understand them for some time now. Crystals vibrate at different frequencies. When we lived without electricity our radio was an old crystal set that broadcasted over the airways. Many magical places also hold this quality and are magical due to their mineral content and vibration. Because crystals vibrate at a higher rate they can be programed to transmit waves of signals that can be used for various purposes such as Magic. They need to be cleared and "awakened" first, I use salt water from the ocean to do that and then gently drop them onto the sand... this awakens them and they are ready for the intent you chose to use them for, usually they are used for transmitting healing or acts to reinforce a desired effect. I have a friend who programed her crystals to aid in weight loss and was very successful.

Salt can be programed...They are tiny crystals.... that's

one of the reasons why I use it to keep snakes away. Plus my Pap always did it so I do it just the way I was taught. When he read the Psalms, he was actually programing the crystals in the salt!!

<u>Graduate of Boarding School</u>

7. You are the product of your rural upbringings in Maryland and your Mother's cosmopolitan consciousness based on her life in France, these very contrasting influences have had what effect upon your life?

As a little kid I didn't know my Mother. She was off some place called Europe or France. She would send me little gifts from Germany and Switzerland. But she was not a real person to me until I was much older. I saw pictures of her and when I was 6 yrs old she came to visit the States for a few weeks. We had a family reunion and I had my picture taken with her before she left again for Paris. She was beautiful and still is at the age of 80 and has beautiful red hair. Only in my later life as a teen did it have an impact on me. She felt that living with my Grandparents was to "old fashioned" and I needed some structure and disciple in my lifestyle. My education became a really big thing at the time. By then my Mother was married to my Step-Father and settled in Alexandria, Va. My Mother and Step-father would travel out West a lot and had friends there. I used to spend my summers between Colorado, Wyoming and Montana. I panned for gold and hit it "rich" by finding a few nuggets from time to time. I had friends out there that I hung around with and once in Montana a full blooded Native American boy got smitten by me and the next year I went out he presented me with a full 10 point rack of elk horns. I still have them, but it is hard to find just the right spot to hang them, if you know what I mean… they are HUGE !!!

When I turned 15, I was sent back to Pennsylvania to Pittsburg to an exclusive all girls' Catholic Prep boarding school which was a part of the Pittsburg Diocese. To make matters worse, it was a school that was connected to a cloistered convent sitting on top of a mountain with NOTHING around it for miles and miles. That became my home until I graduated in the spring of 1967. I went through a bit of culture shock, but all in all it taught me qualities and gave me an inner strength that would I have drawn on throughout the years. Believe me, living with whack-o Nuns hitting you with wooden rulers and rolled up newspapers was not a favorite of mine. AND I was one of the few non Catholic kids there, so I was clueless. None the less, I gave the Nuns a run for their money and had a few kicks and giggles along the way. Survival was the trick, and so I became good at it.

Consequently, I am a combination of my earlier childhood that I still hold dear and close to me, and the Properly Refined Lady as my mother envisioned me to become. My Mother and I are very close now, and I speak with her every day in most cases. We love each other deeply, even if we are from two different worlds.

8. *You have told me of a family member who wore the 'veil' what does that mean?*

As you know my grandfather also had a twin Sister as I have mentioned earlier, they were born in January 1894. When my grandfather was born he had a "Veil" over his face. The veil was carefully removed then carefully kept and placed in the family Bible. The veil is actually called a Caul. It is believed that when a child is born with a veil over their face they hold special and unique properties, like some may have the "sight" and can tell the future, or they have the ability to heal, but importantly they can tap into their inner energy and use it readily to manifest intent, for example his knowledge and aptitude in the use of hexes and cures, which he was known to do. However, it was known from the beginning that my grandfather's abilities were something that was inherited naturally and he was guided by instinct. He had amazing insight and abilities that could be considered along the line of supernatural qualities. There were others in the family with special abilities; actually it runs strong on both my Pap's side and my Grandmother's side. But my Pap was sort of doubled dipped with it.

9 Explain your attraction for the Deitsch, Do you consider yourself one? What are your opinions of the 'Deitsch' magical community?

I never examined or thought of it in those terms. It didn't occur to me one way or another. I came from a family whose roots were forever in Pennsylvania and many of them had strange ways which I learned were full of Hexes on both sides. Words like that were never used in my home. We would "Fix" someone or something or Jinx them, but we never used the word HEX. We knew who and what we were and never discussed it. We were a part of a whole big clan of our relatives living in Pennsylvania and I knew I was closely interwoven and connected to them. I guess I knew I was different because my Pap's nick name was Jinx and my name was a variation of that. His mother knew it when he was born right away because of the veil on his face, and so did the all the old timers. As I mentioned his twin sister my Great Aunt Elda also was gifted.

However, I never connected all the dots or defined myself until recently when I became a member of the Hexenkunst yahoo group owned by Patricia Fisher Neidrich. There I met you Hunter, and when I did, then the memories and the rest of the unspoken things came to light for me to understand through adults eyes. It was like the flood gates opened and even to this day I still remember more and more things that have been long forgotten. All the Elders are now gone and the ones as old as I am in my family did not have the same upbringing and exposure or opportunities as I did. I feel very blessed that my Pap and Aunt Elda took me under their wing and nurtured me with kindness and unconditional love. My grandmother was there with her traditional ways of homemaking, keeping me clean and looking after me like a Mother Hen, forgiving me for all my antics and grief I caused her from worry, and to wash and cut out the globs in my hair before I got old enough to comb It and wrap it in rags to form long curls.

I think a lot of people today who are not of the heritage or blood lines are interested in our culture and want to drink from our fountain. They tend to want to know about our folk ways and especially our folk magic, so they seek out books and the internet to learn about these things. They run on other people's memories and not their own. An example of this is the latest interest in the "old religions" such as Wicca. Much has been written on that subject and many people have embraced it claiming that they are born and raised in that heritage. Largely what they have learned has come straight from books and the internet. Those of us who were brought up around the Pa. Dutch or the Deitsch culture know that our people were very clannish and we were taught things by example and through oral application. For the most part these things that were taught were never written down but handed down. Our traditions can be found in our food and in the way we celebrate holidays. It is represented in our beautiful art and our love of nature. It is ingrained in our consciousness. If you scratch the surface you will find it runs much deeper; a world within itself rich in the tenacity of its people to hold on to their beliefs and customs.

I want to share with you a story about my Aunt Maggie and Uncle Ezra: I think I really began to realize just how strongly my people were connected to the old ways and folk magic was when my oldest daughter was born. My daughter was born with Spina Bifida, or also known as open spine, a severe condition that was virtually untreatable at the time. Experimental work was being done only in specialized hospitals. She was born in Washington D.C. in 1968. Some of the symptoms were an enlarged head caused by water on the brain also known as hydrocephalus, along with the potential to have a severe curvature of the spine or scoliosis. My Pap had died in 1966 so my Grandmother (Mom) was old but still able to get around, she felt it would be good if we made a trip" UP HOME" to see her Aunt Maggie and Uncle Ezra to find out what they could do to help. Aunt Maggie and Uncle Ezra were actually my grandmothers Great Aunt and Uncle. She was 101 years old born in 1868 and Ezra was 103 years old born in 1866. They lived deep up within the Ridges and it took quite a trek to get to their home. We packed up my daughter when she was able to travel and took her to see them. Maggie right away knew there was something very wrong with her, so she put on her apron and began to work on her. She held her close to herself over her shoulder and took her hand and rubbed down her back and spine. She said words that whispered and closed her eyes and prayed and sang that same soft lullaby for what seemed a half hour or so. My daughter was completely relaxed and had fallen asleep in Maggie's arms. Then Maggie handed her over to Uncle Ezra and be began soothing her and gently began his work on her head. He held her in her arms while she was asleep and rubbed the top and sides of her head and ran his hand in front of her face without touching her and blew in her face. She laid in his arms while he prayed and whispered over her. This went on for some time, and then he said, "Mathew, Mark, Luke and John….. Bless this baby mind and soul"……….Amen. Aunt Maggie lifted my baby out of Uncle Ezra's arms and handed my sleeping baby back into my arms and then Maggie went into their kitchen and changed her apron. We were invited to all sit down to some cold buttermilk and homemade bread with sweet apple butter to eat before we headed back over the Ridges.

Shortly thereafter, Aunt Maggie and Uncle Ezra died, but they left behind a miracle. To this day my daughters head is average size and she has normal to above normal intelligence. Also her back is as straight as an arrow. She never required any surgery to correct her posture. She is completely independent but chooses to live with my husband and me. She is now 43 and will turn 44 in October and as healthy as an ox. That was what true Pennsylvania Deisch Magic is about; Devout Love, trust and the power that comes through the Will and true Belief in something much Greater; A Devine Power that is present to work miracle's such as this one. This is only one example of our unique folk faith and magic, and I whole heartily embrace it. It is something that is real and cannot be faked.

I realized I belonged to a very unique and talented family, steeped in old Pa. Dutch folk ways, lore and healing, but what I didn't know what it was called. So to answer your question, I think I hold many of the old folk ways and culture within me. I often talk with Patricia Neidrich, who is a very dear friend of mine and she has a way of tapping into my resources for me to remember those things that have been long forgotten. Hunter Yoder has also been an inspiration to me and he was the first to recognize just where I fit in and who I was. He has a way of bringing out memories that I have that has been deeply buried within my subconscious from the early years of my childhood.

Orva in Pennsylvania Deitsch Mode

10. The kitchen coal range is something that we both have experienced and is very instrumental in Deitsch sympathetic magic, Can you share with us how it was used in your experience?

As I mentioned earlier the twins who were my Grandfather and Great Aunt were born in the middle of January in 1894.They were both kept alive by keeping them warm nested in a shoebox situated in the bun warmer of the old cook stove. But that stove and the one we had when I was growing up was used for other purposes other than cooking food and heating the house. It was also an instrument to manifest magic. The coal bucket was also important factor.

The very first time I actually saw and participated in magic was when I was 5 years old and struggling with the first grade. My teacher was old an maid who liked to intimate children and keep them tight under her rule. One day she had some forms for me to take home so my "Parents" could fill them out and sign them. I did what I was told and took them home and gave them over to Mom. She signed her name and under it she also signed "legal Guardian". Well the next day when I turned the papers to her she reviewed them and called me up to her desk in front of the whole class and wanted to know WHY my MOTHER was unable to sign the papers. At this point I did not know that my grandparents were not my birth parents, so this gave me quite a start and much confusion followed. So the teacher sent the papers home again for my MOTHER OR FATHER to sign them. At this point I was confused so I went to my Pap and asked him what she meant. And this is what he said to me: The next time that ole teacher asks you about your Mother or Father you tell her that a crow shit you out on a stump and the sun hatched you.

The next day I returned to school with the same signatures that bore "Legal Guardian" on them. The teacher wanted to know what the meaning of this was, it was a direct order. So, in my defense I recited exactly what my Pap had told me to say. To tell the truth I thought that ole woman was about to lay an egg, she got all red faced and grabbed me by the top of my hair and took me over to the sink and washed my mouth out with green soap. Afterwards she took me into the hall and yelled at me while slamming my head against the concrete block wall. Then she brought me inside the class room and tied me to a chair and sat me in a corner. By this time I was really losing it. I began to cry and then I peed myself till it ran into my bobby socks and into my new shoes. Finally when recess came and she was not watching me, I undid myself and got as far away from that ole school as fast as my legs could carry me. . I was familiar with all the woods around there so I cut my way home the back way.

When my Pap found me I was home sitting on a stack of cinder block outside the coal bin crying. He asked me what was wrong and I told him the story. Next thing I knew my Pap yelled, "Get in the car Martha" so my grandmother responded to the request without haste. She didn't even have time to take off her apron by the time we went to school. I sat in the hall for a long time while my Pap and Mom was in the Office. Afterwards my Pap put his hat back on and we got back into the '36Plymouth and headed for home.

Much later that night is when the magic began. It was along about midnight when he called me to him out of bed and told me we were going to "fix" that ole teacher to mind her own business. He gave me a piece of paper bag and he had one too. We wrote the teachers name on the bag and then wrote my name overtop of hers. We folded the paper very carefully until it was a little square and then he stoked up the ole cook stove till it was good and a blaze. He said some words over the papers, ones that I had never heard before and ones that I will never forget. Then we cast our papers into the hot flames. He sat in his rocking chair with me on his lap and we bit off a plug of chewing tobacco and chewed it then spit the tobacco into the coal bucket to set the seal. The next day when I went to school the teacher was nowhere to be found and we got a new teacher to take her place. Years later I found out that she retired and never went back to teaching from that day onward.

Other strange occurrences happened in our neighborhood when a form of abuse went unchecked. Our cat came home one day horribly mutated. Pap nursed him back to health, but his sister cat that lived next door died from the same grave injuries. This was very upsetting and my Pap had a good idea who was behind it because there was a man who lived down the street that raised a flock of pigeons and blamed the cats for getting inside the cages, killing his birds, when it was actually rats. So my Pap once again "fixed" the situation. A few weeks later when the old man was not at home, his house burned to the ground including his pigeon coop. No one was surprised and there was no remorse in the neighborhood. All the pet cats and animals were safe from the hands of evil doings.

The Fire Department came out and investigated the fire to find its cause. It was noted that the fire was caused by combustion from all the piles of pigeon poop and noted that no signs of arson was evident.

My Grandparents always were great supporters of the Fire Department due to the amount of trees and underbrush around our homes living in the woods. Things could burn out of hand very quickly and the Fire Company was always on alert. So my Grandparents always bought tickets for their annual Spaghetti Dinner, but we never went to them because Spaghetti was Italian food and that was considered foreign food and such food was never allowed to grace our table.

Our kitchen wood stove cooked a many of good meals for us and served us well over the years of my youth. It also warmed our clothing in the winter time and the oven was a good place to put our cold feet into after a day of sled riding. It seemed that my early years centered around the old kitchen cook stove and for good reason. It too became a great part of my security and I found much comfort associated with it and the people who tended its fire and banked its coals.

11. Hoodoo magic and Hexerei, part and parcel or one in the same?

NO. . They are two completely different things. They may have similar qualities but their backgrounds come from a different blend of culture and ideology. I believe our German Hexeri has had some influence on Hoodoo in its development as the Native Americans had influence on our German practices when our ancestors came to this wilderness called America. However, our folk ways are very different and its methodology stems from a wide scale European tribal point of view that pre dates Christianity and resonates from prehistoric times.

I think for more in-depth study on the subject of Hoodoo, Catherine Yronwode's book, <u>Hoodoo Herb and Root Magic: A Material Magica of African-American Conjure</u>, would be an outstanding read.

12. I know you have lived in Florida and Key West for quite some time And we both know Miami.. What are some of your favorite Latin dishes?

My grandmother would do a lot of canning and I learned the art of canning and cooking it at her knee. When I a married, I married into a very old Southern Maryland family. So I had to learn how to cook Southern style. We grew our own food and had fruit trees and grape arbors we made wine from, and also how to get into the Spirit of things. His family had many hidden culinary secrets which I was sworn to secrecy. When our kids came along, they too were raised in the style and mind set of the way we were raised by our grandparents. (My husband was also raised by the old ways by his grandparents who were all from Southern Maryland) However, the way we were both raised was very similar. We both shared peculiar childhoods, often humorous and rich with family folk lore. North meets the South.

So from cooking strictly Pa. Dutch style to cooking Southern and Cajun style I have come a long way. Since moving to the Florida Keys 17 years ago, I learned to cook a lot of Latin Dishes and my family loves them. We have different kinds of vegetables from the Caribbean as well as fresh spices and roots. Flavors here are like the weather and its people, colorful and spicy. A huge variety of seafood is fresh from our beautiful turquoise waters and easily obtained. I like to cook Cuban style quite often, I guess because of the Cuban influence here and the blending of Latin culture has become ingrained in our way of cooking comfort foods. I love to cook Cuban Roast Pork with black beans and yellow rice w/ rope fried plantains (that grow in my back yard) on the side. I love the spice and taste of real oxtail soup, simmered all day. From Barbados I love how they jerk meat and leaned to cook Marconi Cheese Pie a 4 inch high dish of pure cheese and spice and mixed with macaroni. Seafood is fresh here and I have caught some very strange critters that I have set loose into the Ocean, but I like to use ALL the fish. When I get done cleaning it I save the head and spine and cook it all down to make a wonderful Fish stew. Paella is a gift from the Gods. I cook it from fish head stock and add chicken and pork and seafood into it. I make my own Sofida and add to it with saffron and yellow rice along with tomatoes and chili's and squid or octopus chopped fine. Of course Key West Lobster and Kew West pink shrimp is for Kings and melts in your mouth.

We have an abundance of good food here from many cultures. Believe me… WE EAT GOOD Here; and LIFE IS SO VERY GOOD. I AM BLESSED.

13. Any thoughts on Sex magic?

I have been having sex magic with my husband for over 42 plus years. We are so bonded emotionally and physically that sex is something that joins us together as one spiritually. Sex never gets old or boring, sex is alive and a necessity in a healthy relationship between two people who love each other deeply and the magic is always a key part of things. From the beginning of time, sex has been the driving force that runs the world and all its creatures. Sex is a part of Divinity that each of us hold. Without sex creation would cease to exist. My views on sex between married couples are a joining of souls. As a single person, sex can and is fun, I have been there and done that and it was just that: FUN and Creative… however, now of days I strongly recommend "safe sex". None the less even though as a single person in all its excitement, I feel it lacks the sanctity of love and trust and bonding.

I am old fashioned in that to have trust you must make a true commitment to each other and to the Gods, pledging respect and honesty to one another in their presence. With the right partner sex ultimately generates sex magic. It opens up a different world that that only belongs to you and your mate, even after years of marriage… Sex Magic is still ongoing, intimately creative and exciting, full flavored lust that comes only off the top shelf of Life.

Vielen Dunka Hunter.

Lch freue mich, Hunter....Dunka

Orva

O. Henrietta Fisher Interview with Hunter Yoder

Hex + Sex (2012)

1. ***Heil O. Henrietta, tell us about your sexual connection with your art, and/or what is it about sex that makes you want make art about it?***

Everything about sex and intimacy makes me want to make art about it!!!! From the childlike bliss of a new lover to the devastation of losing a love! I find that my sexuality is the core of my being; everything that goes right or goes wrong is traced back to sex and sexuality. As a 30 year-old woman, and a new mother, I decided that it was high time to stop fooling myself that I should make art about anything else! Sexuality is what I know- what I am experienced in! From the moment I started my first piece in my series "Playa vs. Puma" I felt a pulsating, raw, and impatient force pulling me towards telling my story of sex, love and loss.

My sexual connection to my art is that it is completely raw and honest about my life and my loves. I have always written about my experiences with love and sex, but these are the first images that I have created about my experiences. The work is autobiographical, which I feel gives it the real power! I needed to tell my story in order to finally rid myself of some demons as well as elevate my artwork and sexuality. I'm sorting all of my personal passion, anger, love, and resentment out each time I create a piece. Sometimes I go over the image again and again just trying to bring to the surface psychological remedies. It's art therapy at its highest effectiveness!!!!

Until recently, I have always felt that my sexuality was actually an inadequacy. In my previous relationships or sexual encounters, I was made to feel like I was too sexually needy or never satisfied. As though it were a curse preventing me from being a good, satisfied girlfriend, lover or wife! I blamed myself for being emotionally unavailable and thought that my deeply cut abandonment issues were the reason that I replaced intimacy with sex. However, very recently, through this body of work "Playa vs. Puma" I realized that all of that was bullshit! It was others trying to scapegoat their own inadequacies onto me and push me down while they built themselves up.

Finding a new appreciation for my fine-tuned sexuality and the joy within me, I feel more powerful and happy than I have ever in my life!

2. ***You were/are doing larger panels with colored chalk that have a very painterly look about them, From talking with you earlier you described how they were sort of an exorcism of personal demons from the past which haunted you in your sleep. Could you take us through that period?***

Exorcism is exactly what it was! Basically the short version is that I married very young, 22… I met a likeminded artist/musician from Baltimore and left college, my family, and my home to live with him. I tried desperately to fit my round peg into his square hole that he carved out for me. As many of us children of divorce do, I struggled painfully to overcompensate for his shortcomings and hold our marriage together. He was very nasty at times, made me feel like I was a whore for wanting to make love to him, and constantly tore me down about how I was a bad "feminist", I was still painfully devoted to him. I had replaced my father's emotional abuse with my husband's.

Music was our common ground and connection. Music was the most important thing in both of our lives. I was photographing punk/hardcore bands at the time- all the time. He was a musician with several projects going at once.

Anyone that has met me or knows me will usually use "happy" as a word to describe me. Indeed joy is something that tends to radiate from within me. I smile all the time and enjoy life and people... He was quite the opposite, very dark and very tortured.

Both Aquarius, we grew apart, more independent of each other and no longer feeding off of the creative energy from one another. My husband suffered from undiagnosed (at the time) bipolar disorder. He was pulling me into his black hole of depression and hate. I felt like I was being drowned... my sexuality shriveled up from constant rejection, my body image melted as I sculpted my faux-pregnant silhouette, my joy was extinguished! My family begging me to leave him at Christmas 2005, as he was locked in the bathroom of our apartment threatening suicide, I made a mad dash for the door in fear that he would take me with him to my death!

I moved back to Philadelphia and quickly found myself again. Though it was extremely painful to force myself away from the man I considered my soul mate, it was very necessary. But I pined for him still…. Up until this year, I thought of him often and literally dreamt of him every night…. He was absolutely haunting me!

So if it was so bad and so painful why the fuck couldn't I shake it?? This is precisely what I am trying to figure out, however having a new love, someone who believes in me and holds me up high, this has helped rid me of traces of inadequacy that he cut deeply in me.

Leverage {puma} (2011)

3. *Currently you are mixing Pa German Hexology into your work, what happened there?*

I met you Hunter! When David Stanley Aponte brought me to The Hex Factory for the first time in July, and I saw the show of Pennsylvania German Hex Signs by Hexologists, Hunter Yoder, Patricia Hall, and Jakob Brunner, I felt instantly attracted to the images, the process and the purpose.

Particularly the vision of your work and the obvious power radiating from the images. As I got to know you and your work better, I was more and more impressed with your radically forward thinking vision that brought an old tradition of our ancestors back to life with a modern twist only built for the willful and fierce among us! It was the rebellion of it all that really drew me in to the work, and the care and delicacy for which you treated such a magical tradition of our PA German ancestors. I found myself much more excited by your work and process than anything I had seen happening in the art world. I thought that both you and your work were totally badass!!

When we first met you said something about my work that I've never forgotten, "The work is very good and hot! Creative energy and sexual energy are the same thing....." I was very impressed with the fact that you instantly got what I was intending to do with the work. I didn't need to explain my intention; it was fantastic to have someone so aesthetically aligned with my vision and execution. At that moment I realized that my work was more than art- in a sense my 4 ft square boards were actually hex signs (obviously non-traditional), but they were executed with an intent and purpose, and I used Sex Magic (the only means by which I know) to attain these goals.

I am very proud of my Pennsylvania German heritage, and my maternal grandmother certainly has a magical presence about her. The whole picture seemed to focus for me when my worlds of art and family collided! When I made my first hex sign- it felt like coming home, warmth and familiarity to the process, as though I had done it many many times before.

Since my show at The Hex Factory, I have turned my art making attention to hex signs about sex, fertility and love. Certainly I can harness some of my sexual potency and share it through my "painted prayers" for better sex for others!

4. *Can you talk about 'Sex Magic' in your work?*

Sex Magic is something that I recall learning about as a teen when I best friend, Heather, was dabbling in witchcraft and reading everything there was to read about magic. I was a very restless teenager with a body built for a woman! I was wasting a lot of good pussy on bad lovers, and my promiscuity got the best of me. Devoured from the pain of losing "love". I didn't connect the dots that I was practicing Sex Magic until recently with a new lover, but I believe that in my early days (teenage years-twenties) I was desperately seeking an outlet for my potent sexual energy, I was not disciplined enough, at the time, to use that energy, through orgasms, to get what I needed and wanted. I became caught up in the games of love and didn't concentrate on the potential power of it!

I am still learning about the practice and powers of Sex Magic with my lover. The sex is elevated on so many different levels, that I have never previously experienced, I was so high and so perplexed when we first made love. I did my homework and realized that we had both tapped into our Sex Magic capabilities. I realized that he guided me through my first concentrated efforts of Sex Magic. Through his gaze, I took his lead and proceeded to lead us both towards my will and intentions. We both set a goal without a word spoken. I have never had a lover look into my eyes and pierce my core quite this way. It has been the most satisfying sex I have ever experienced, and has touched every aspect of my life including, and most predominantly, my artwork.

"At the moment of orgasm, it is important to direct your entire concentration and desire to your goal, willing it. Visualize the orgasmic energy in the form of a beam, ball or vortex, penetrating the object/person, lighting it up with a brilliant aura of energy that is programmed."

5. *You have Deitsch and Welsh lineage, what effect does your ancestry have in the work of O. Henrietta Fisher?*

My Deitsch and Welsh lineage have heavily influenced me. As you know dear, the Deitsch women can be quite stubborn, powerful and relentless!!! As with my Welsh ladies! We are not meek and mild, by any means! I love that about my heritage! The women are very powerful and very willful! I try to channel this willfulness, especially when I am feeling weak and hurt.

All of the artwork that I make I consider an homage to my family. It is impossible for me to ignore the parallels of their stories of love, sex and power to my own story. I have been so blessed to be surrounded my powerful women for my entire life!! I was raised with a spirit of not taking shit and not backing down from what I want!

6. *Give us the rundown of your recent show at THE HEX FACTORY.*

It was an exhibit of my most recent series, "Playa vs. Puma" (2011). This work reflects intimate moments, within a sexual relationship, where power is shifted, slightly or drastically, between partners. However small or large the shift may be, the effects are palpable and set the stage for the next rumble. This body of work is particularly based on my exploration into why myself, and others, compete with each other for power in a relationship, and the power struggles (however subtle or blatant) that ensue. The lines between truth-present, past, fantasy tend to blur in my work.

The institution rejected this work, it was labeled too sexually charged for the bureaucratic niche of Tyler School of Art. It's art school for fucks sake- really? I was pissed and I was determined! I pitched the idea to my dear friend, David Stanley Aponte if he would curate a show of this work! As an art rebel himself, he said he would be interested and told me we just needed to find the right fit.

With no trace of coincidence, I found myself on the steps of The Hex Factory one July afternoon. As I walked in to the space, "Cherry Bomb" blaring, I knew I had found a home for my work and my vision. It didn't take much convincing when you and I met and I showed you my work. You got it- immediately! I was told my David that you both were giving me a solo show straight away! And the rest is history baby!

Honored and humbled by the high regard for my work and my practices, I have found the dynamic between us to be extremely inspiring and positive. I appreciate the feedback about my work and for once feel that someone is actually invested in my success rather than my demise! Gives me strength to push back against the opposition of my work!

7. *Ms O. Henrietta, tell us about your recent interest in handguns. Why should women carry?*

Guns are fucking sexy, and a symbol of power and protection, not unlike the rosette! The first time I've ever shot a gun was a few weeks ago at a local shooting range. I was so distracted by all of the other shots being fired, that I decided to use the same method that I use with sex magic; that is that I visualized my goal (hitting the target, or close) and squeezed the trigger tight, light I squeeze my kegals during an orgasm, and bam- I hit the target! I used my intuition, set a goal and let the power of my intent do that rest! Powerful stuff, hitting bull's-eyes with my eyes closed! I also love the feeling of my cold steel Ruger LC9 tucked against my warm, white bosom.

This is a new era baby! I'm not the kind of woman that likes to take a backseat and let someone else fight for my causes or protect me… we are a new breed, inner-city hexologists, taking back the city, reclaiming our ancestral fertile ground! If the powers that be won't ensure my child's safety- and mine I sure as fuck will!!!

So fucking tired of the chickenheads in the sticks chirping away on line pretending that they are fighting for something, when really they're just tucked away safely out of harms way. The real changes are happening right here in the Ghetto. On the front line of the fight is where I want to be!

Fisher & Yoder Hex Portraits (2012)

8. *Some traditionalists have voiced concerns about the direction your Hexes have taken, what is your response?*

How much more traditional can you get than being the descendant of the Fisher's of the Fisher House in Oley,

PA? My family is still in Berks County. I am using Hexology as a vehicle to create sex magical objects.... This is a practice of Hexerei, Germanic pre-Christian Witchcraft.

I am growing accustomed to the puritanical sensibility of the Monokultur of today. Just like in "Beliefs and Superstitions of the Pennsylvania Germans", by Edwin M. Fogel, 1915, a 410 page document which has the full spectrum of folk beliefs on every aspect of life and death of the Deitsch, I was devastated but certainly not surprised to discover that the chapter on 'Sex' had been completely deleted.

Sex is power and a powerful fertility goddess is now queen of the Hex Factory!

9. *What is 'die besten' making love or making art about making love? Or is the boundary between them blurred in your work?*

What a great question Hunter... I believe it depends on the partner- many times, making art about sex has been much more satisfying than making love with someone who just can't quite measure up. However, for me personally, my ultimate lover is someone who was aligned with my vision of making art about making love, and we could do it together, as part of our process of lovemaking and art making. Where the line between our bodies and our images are eliminated.

I believe I have found this, finally, and it is truly magical! Elevating my loving, my fucking, and my artwork!

O.Henrietta interviews Hunter Yoder for the show,"In Between the Sheets at the Hex Factory, Hunter Yoder and O. Henrietta Fisher"

Heiden Hexologists, O Henrietta Fisher and Hunter Yoder

1. You have written about being an inner city Hexologist, can you elaborate on your interest in bringing Hexology and your practices to the city?

   Its my position that the new frontier so to speak is the urban inner city. My move to East Kensington, Philadelphia was to appreciate the place that was the portal for most of the German immigration into America, Philadelphia really is German, Germantown is the first German settlement in North America.

   Growing up in Berks County, Philadelphia was the big city. I live in a very German, Polish, Scotch, Irish, Welsh neighborhood. People are frequently surprised to learn this. The urban areas are being reclaimed by the ancestors of those who originally built the neighborhoods. As decimated as these neighborhoods have become, the Germans are back rebuilding and appreciating in value these neglected buildings. The statement I am making is that if you do not value your neighborhood enough to invest in it and make it better, I will eat your lunch......

1. Tell us about this new lady in your life? She seems to have had an influence on your work and interest in Sex Magic.

   When O. Henrietta Fisher and I met for the first time it was pretty apparent that it was our Orlog to do so. It caught a lot of attention, there seemed to be a great interest in keeping us apart. It was pretty clear what was going to happen. This is some pretty powerful stuff. We both have very old ancestral roots in the Pa Deitsch community in Berks County. O. Henrietta was not up to speed regarding the recent explosion in the interest in Pa German Magic. She wasn't aware that she was a very special person in this regard. It was clear to me that she was a hereditary Hex on both sides of the family. She certainly is far easier on the eyes then the Deitsch girls I was accustomed to. She has an equal amount of the Welsh on both sides. I never had a Welshie before......I took it upon myself to educate her in these matters.

3. How do you envision your hex work evolving in the next year?

   The Hex work seems to evolve by itself. Like acquiring the knowledge of the Runes, it is important to be patient and let the Hexology speak to you. One thing leads to another. Besides the Runic influence on the traditional Deitsch barnstars, I have been influenced by numerology, sex magic, and the Galdrstaves of prechristian Iceland. The possibilities are endless.

4. You seemed drawn to my work because it may have reminded you of your goddess art work from the 80's- what is it like painting sex from a male perspective?

   You might be surprised to find that it is very similar to your very feminine perspective, yeah its all about the female body some male imagery but definitely not as interesting as your 'body' of work. I worked with geometic shapes and patterns many times using fluorescent colors to imitate the heightened, altered state I experienced when having some really good sex. I found it interesting that we both used pornography as a basis for some of the work. I used it for the various 'configurations' to create a very basic design to house my patterns and colors.

   Good art like good sex has a visceral feeling and when it has that its good and hot. The feeling persists everytime you look at it.

5. The Hex Factory gallery has been open now, showing work, since Summer 2011- what are some of the future events, artists that you have in mind for the gallery?

   Well really Dave Aponte was handling most of the programming but he has moved to Berlin, Germany to further his career in the visual arts. We are happy about this because clearly it is good for not only him but The Hex Factory, which focuses on the Germanic tribal arts and Deitsch Hexology. Currently you and I are doing a 'Between the Sheets' show which takes the Germanic tribal arts to the bedroom....its gonna be pretty good.

6. As a fertility god, what is it like to fuck/make love? Are there separate intentions set other than pleasure like with Sex Magic?

   I can't seem to separate fucking, love making and sex magic. When you and I began 'seeing' each other, we really had no other choice, nor did we desire another option. Sex magic functions several ways, besides operating as a great way to send an intention it initially usually involves 'charming' You recall the 'White armed woman' Runic charm I used on you to turn your thoughts towards me. Another basic method to possess a lover is for the partner to have the 'taste' of the others sex in his or her mouth and then to kiss the other on mouth. As you have taught me, bodily fluids are very powerful magical tools.

Of course the most important sex magical intention is to impregnate the woman. This is done intentionally by both. That is what its all about, really. Sex Magic to impregnate creates magical children....

Runic Cock Hex, 2012 Fisher/Yoder

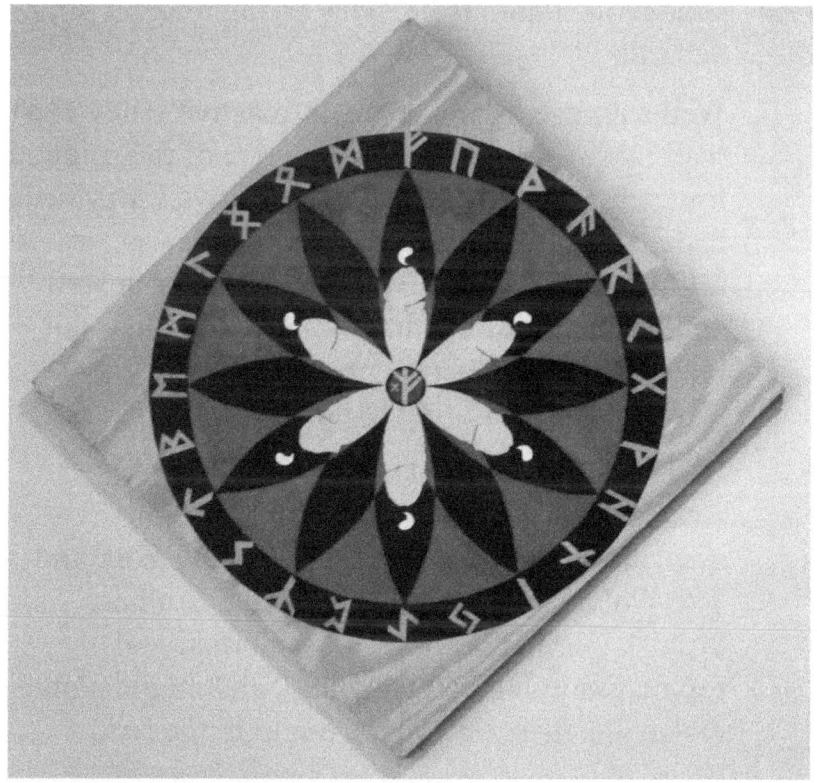

7. You are a avid cyclist, you have spoken about it being a meditative time for you.... how does this influence your work? Do you plan hexes while on the bike?

   Cycling besides being good for your body is really good for the mind. It develops an ability to focus and strengthens the will. It also gives you an extended period of time to work things out. I do workout problems I am having on a Hex or perhaps 'see' a new one.

8. It appears that you are no longer a part of the Der Heidevolkstamm tribe, what brought about your departure?

   Well supposedly my status is 'inactive' They can't really throw me out since I am one of the original founders of the tribe. Hey who knows I may be back with them before you know it. I was informed of my inactive status by Patricia Hall another founding member after it was clear our relationship of several years was over. I guess it was the practical thing to do. These things happen.

   Besides Der Heidevolksstamm, I have an association with the Irminfolk in New York and The Wolves of Vinland in Virginia. Both are Folkish Germanic tribes. My international reputation in Heiden Hexology and magic plants makes this tribal tiff just a bump in the road.

9. Give us a preview of what will be in the new

book?

The book consists of published and unpublished essays on what I call now, Heiden Hexology. Heiden is Deutsch for heathen. I've written pretty extensively on Hexerei or Germanic witchcraft based on my experiences growing up in Berks County. This area of thought has become a battlefield in recent years due to the interest in it because it is the only continuous European magical tradition in the New World. So I guess I've pissed on my territory making sure the facts of my culture are right. The book also includes interviews with both Hexologists and Rune magicians and well German witches or Hexes. Of course, the book will have a lot of my own Hex signs, many of them very original. I have the perspective that these 'signs' are magical objects connected to a very old Germanic tradition which goes back as far as ancient India which is where our Indo European ancestors originated.

10. Finally, how can a woman (me) keep a God (you) satisfied?

What every god wants, to be worshipped!

I think it is more a matter of fate, timing, and the magical attractive force that brought us together. The intense focus we have on each other is certainly important. I think we both feel safe in this love we share, this is true when we are apart. You know what I want.....give it to me!

666. You are very outspoken about women arming themselves, tell us your thoughts on packing heat....

Well we live in a lawless, dangerous society. Law enforcement really is interested in only issuing parking tickets and such. I recently received a ticket for running a red light on a bicycle, fine, $120. Illegals pour into this country. Minority subcultures prey upon the educated middle class. Number one mark by criminals , is white women. These lowlifes have no respect for women and they are cowards. I find that an appalling indicator of how well multiculturalism has worked. As a father, a husband, a lover of my women, I want them to be able to use a gun to defend themselves because clearly no one else is when I am not around. I like that it empowers women. They feel on an equal footing and there is no need for them to take a lot of unwanted and dangerous sexist shit. Carrying a weapon requires responsible behavior, this is not a game anymore.

'Milton Hill Goddess Hex,' Hunter Yoder, 2011

999. You identify yourself as a radical traditionalist, break it down....

Radical traditionalism refers to the renaissance in Germanic 'paganism' I view it through my usual Pa German lense as the reindigenization of my folk. The magical traditions I grew up with in Berks County are the legacy of our European forefathers. That is our tradition. Revitalizing it, reanimating it and rejecting multiculturalism and the petroleum fueled "monokultur" is the radical part, advanced thinking is being done today by such 'traditionalists' all over the world.

Reviews at the Hex Factory

Between the Sheets

O. Henrietta and Hunter Yoder at the Hex Factory

Working within the Folk Art context of Hexology one is struck by thr myriad of 'pretenders, outlanders and scallywags,' who populate cyberspace.......

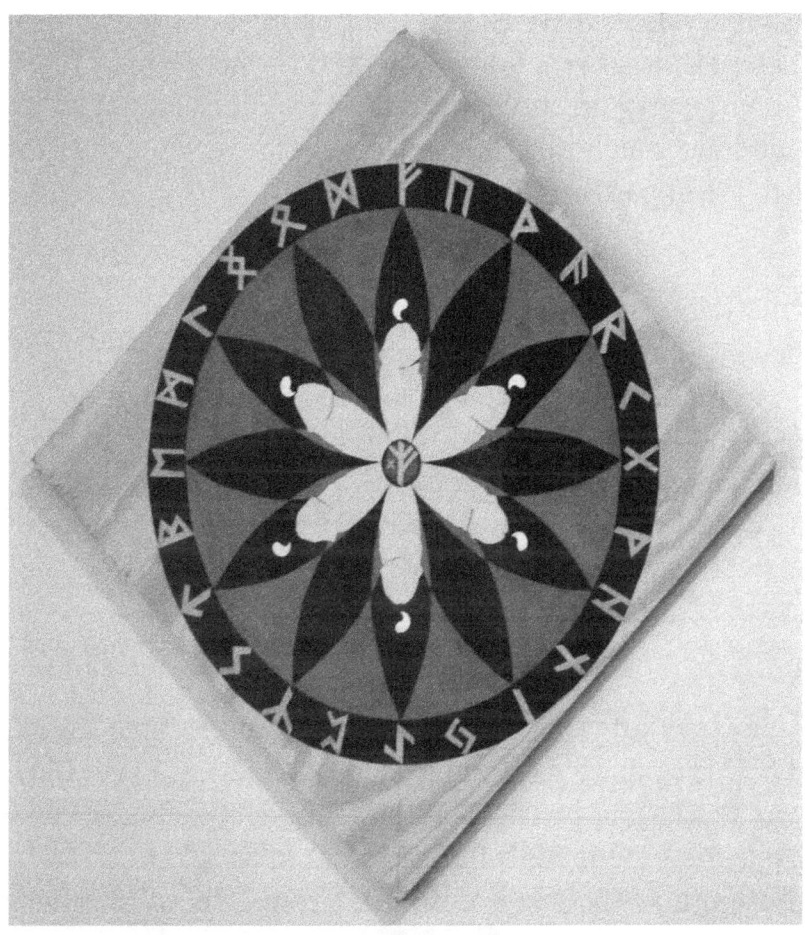

'Sex Magic Hex,' Fisher/Yoder 2012

However, it is unusual to find those from the 'kultur' using the craft to expand the possibilities, extend the idiom, in other words innovate, backed by legitimate geographical and ancestral ties to bring the form out of the mire of cheap Pa Dutch Hex Sign dot com fixes that stink like the Philadelphia Streets.

IN BETWEEN THE SHEETS, is a breakout show! It leaves all other practitioners behind! In fact it leaves contemporary art in the dust as well. Yoder may have found his match this time. O Henrietta has led Yoder to still 'green pastures'

Sex Magic is a volatile practice, a life long pursuit, focusing on getting it just right. O Henrietta's rapid evolution from large chalks and paint on distressed plywood panels of sex coupling have given way to Gandee-esque Hexes filled with phallic rosettes and menstrual blood. How and why this happened is a very interesting story. I'm not going to kiss and tell however....just listen.

Yoder's end of it is of interest. The show features several of his 'sex paintings' from the early Nineties. From his own admission, he replaced nude models with porno magazine pinups for what he refers to as 'configurations'. One is entitled, 'From Behind' another 'Amor Selvage' or Savage Love. The psychedelic patterns, colors and geometrically shaped panel composites Yoder used to simulate the altered states experienced while engaging in coitus. Not your usual folk art imagery.

Enter the wonderful world of magically charged objects. Both artists/practitioners, to use a graduate school term, 'reference' Lee R. Gandee, a Hexenmeister or master

German witch. His Hex work influence both Yoder and Fisher. This ain't Kansas anymore, folks.

The other major component in the work is the Elder Futhark, the Runes. Magical Germanic signs and symbols which Yoder has incorporated into his Hexology since 2007. Yoder published his essay,' Runic Symbology in Contemporary Deitsch Hexology' in HEX MAGAZINE, Issue Four in Fall 2008. The resulting avalanche of Heathens participating in the practice of Hexology has been significant, most recently documented in, Yoder's piece in HEX MAGAZINE, Issue Nine, entitled, 'Six Six Six' or 'Six Questions to Six Heathen Hexologists and their Six Hexes'.

O' Henrietta's work operates in a very direct way, no symbols or abstracted patterns and shapes simulating sex. Her powerful images tend to kick the inhibited viewer in the teeth, but they really are just an unfiltered expression of endless sweetness, love, don't you know? Totally heterosexual, her 'work' confronts the vulnerability of the viewer who is challenged into the role of participant. Will he or she, 'measure up'?

In particular, the last piece in the show which is a joint effort, a painting which exemplifies an intention done by this sex magic pair, entitled, Hex Magic' features O Henrietta's iconic cock rosette in a background of a twelve pointed rosette, the border features the Elder Futhark, done by Yoder and a central bind rune, a powerful combination of runes in this case Fehu and Algiz with Gebo within the central red 'dot'. Cum issues forth from the six cocks as familiar 'raindrops' reminiscent in the Barnstars of northern Berks County. Numerologically, the Hex expands outward from the six-pointed cock to the twelve-pointed rosette to the twenty-four Runes of the Elder Futhark.

Take these seemingly disparate elements, Folk Art, American Abstract Art, Germanic Magic, Sex Magic, Feminism and genuine Pa German ancestry and combine them in the white ghetto setting of Philadelphia's East Kensington section and now you're starting to sense how dangerous this show really is.

These 'practioners' aren't fucking around, they are angry, armed, and extremely dangerous to the currently accepted standards of 'emerging art,' so called culture in Amerika and the world which they seek to conquer by any means necessary.

Hunter Yoder, Heiden Hexologist
02/21/2012

The new King and Queen of Hexology

Heiden Hexology in Oley, PA

The work of native Berks County Hexologist, Hunter Yoder found its way to Oley via the backdoor, at a place called 'Clay on Main' a delightfully ancient architectural structure on Main Street, Oley.
Hunter Yoder in many ways is the 'prodigal son'

returning with a truck full of fertilizer and diesel fuel to his origins. His Heiden Hexology is not what is seen painted on Barns there. His childhood and young manhood on the farm near Virginville, (the Reading Eagle calls Richmond Township) has yielded a vast folkish spiritual watershed.

His combination of the Hexology of Johnny Ott and others that he grew up with and the addition of the Icelandic Galdrstaves, Germanic magical signs, has created quite a stir in the Germanic Heathen Community. His essays published in periodicals such as

Hex Magazine, out of Portland, Oregon and The Journal of Contemporary Heathen Thought as well as his own published book, entitled, "The Backdoor Hexologist" have established this Yoder on the cutting edge of the new approach to Deitsch kultur. His folk magical approach is unforgivably direct.

Hunter incorporates certain plants and animals into his Hexology. They are chosen specifically for their magical attributes. Hunter has replaced the traditional tulip with a Datura Stramonium Flower. He prefers red roosters over gold finches or Distelfinks.
Instead of the traditional raindrops on the eight pointed stars found on barns, Yoder uses, red ones to symbolize blood.
In this show, we see cross like configurations, not Christian but rather referring to the sun, or Sonnenkreuz. The first is five Hexes the traditional ones, the other is five that Yoder has ceated in the new Heiden form. Hex spirals, Schwarze Sonnes, Niger Bilsenkrauts Hexes, Geilskimmel hexes, the Icelandic *ægishjálmr* combined with his traditional eight pointed Berks county star

his signature departure from the Claypooles, Ivan Hoyts, Zooks etc.

Yes, Yoder has ascended into Hex Godhood. He is no longer a mere mortal Hexologist.

And this show proves it. His hook into the eternal is fertility, the traditional need for the sympathetic Deitsch magic that we all love and know is true in our hearts. Through this ability to grow and wax he has tapped into both the ancient riverbed of folk magic and the new need for those of European descent's reindigenization, tribalism. A response, a rejection to our supposedly multicultural globalized digitized world.

Gottinen und Heiden Hexology

Hunter Yoder at the Hex Factory, November 4 through December 31, 2011

As a special Yuletide treat, Heiden Hexologist, Hunter Yoder has combined the most recent Hexes never before seen in Philadelphia with some of his Goddess creations from the past and present. The inclusion of the Goddesses usually as a part of a Hex design is to reacquaint the public/viewer with his Heiden (Heathen) polytheistic belief structure .The Germanic prechristian pantheon of gods and goddesses and their magical alphabet known as the Elder Futhark of Runes in Pennsylvania German Hexology defines Hunter Yoder's work. Especially exciting is his newest 'Sonne Kreuz' or sun cross.

2011

'Old Europe Goddess,' 2010

Some of the goddess objects reference even earlier neolithic deities from Old Europe, an area formerly known as Yugoslavia extending eastward into the Ukraine and Black Sea as per Marija Gimbutas, famed anthroplogist and author of "Goddesses and Gods of Old Europe". At this time, the Ice Age denied access to most of Europe to the West. The goddesses here are known simply as 'Bird Goddess', and Snake Goddess'. His largest object on display combines several of these neolithic deities into one.

Some of his earlier goddess objects refer to the Canaanite deity, Asherah, as a tree flanked by 'rampant caprids' feeding upon her branches. The Hebrew menorah is a stylization of the asherah. Unfortunately the asherah was cast out of the Temple according to the Torah.

'Blue Asherah,' 2007

Still yet another object refers to the Brazilian deity Jemanja the Makumba fertility goddess. Hunter encountered her at Ubu Praia, a beach just south of Bahia on a trip to Brasil in 2007. Using her energy, he transformed her into a mermaid which surprisingly populates Deitsch imagery. The reference goes back to Europe and the water sprites and river mermaids/sirens of the Rhine.

'Ubu Praia,' 2007

The new Hex work contains completely original motifs that are back in Philadelphia after being on view at the

"Folkish Summer Hallowing" a Germanic Heathen event near Milford, Pa and most recently a monumental show in Oley, PA where this new form of Heiden Hexology was on view for the first time in Berks County. Oley is usually associated with Pow Wow magic, a form of Hexerei.

The goddesses and Deitsch Hexology are vehicles to ensure fertility, something that is taken for granted and maybe even feared today as it was feared by post neolithic cultures that embraced monotheism in the middle east. The early goddess cultures had a far different world view then the later male warrior societies that have dominated the history of man on earth. Their world view was not one of plundering, conquering, and exploiting but rather a participation in life in which the earth/universe is a single living breathing entity. This is the view subscribed to in this show of magical objects.

Hunter Yoder, 10/26/2011

www.ingramcontent.com/pod-product-compliance
Lightning Source LLC
Chambersburg PA
CBHW031133160426
43193CB00008B/127